CHRISTIAN LIVING SERIES

~ Volume 2 ~

Christian Living Series

~ Volume 2 ~

Spiritual Concepts

by His Grace Bishop Youanis

ST SHENOUDA'S MONASTERY
SYDNEY, AUSTRALIA
2012

Christian Living Series - Volume 2
SPIRITUAL CONCEPTS

COPYRIGHT © 2012
St. Shenouda Monastery

All rights reserved. Except for brief quotations in critical publications or reviews, no part of this book may be reproduced in any manner without prior written permission from the publisher.

ST SHENOUDA MONASTERY
8419 Putty Rd,
Putty, NSW, 2330
Sydney, Australia

www.stshenoudamonastery.org.au

ISBN 13: 978-0-9873400-1-6

All scripture quotations, unless otherwise indicated, are taken from the New King James Version®. Copyright © 1982 by Thomas Nelson, Inc. Used by permission. All rights reserved.

Cover Design:
Hani Ghaly,
Begoury Graphics
begourygraphics@gmail.com

Contents

Humility	*7*
Pride	*47*
Dignity	*83*
The Life of Submission	*105*
The Principle of the Narrow Gate	*117*

Humility

"Whoever refuses to enter through the Door of Humility will not find the pasture; and whoever wants to enter from somewhere else is a thief"
(St John Climacus)

- What is Humility?
- Humility in the Lord's life and the lives of His saints
- Humility is the foundation of all virtues
- What does Humility do?
- How can we obtain Humility?
- Practical aspects of humility?

What is humility?

It is not just an outer appearance like wearing simple clothes or talking in a low voice or always lowering the eyes and looking downwards. It is not just words that a person repeats about himself in front of others like saying he is a sinner or unworthy. It is not just phrases said in prayer about one's unworthiness or lowliness. If it was just that, then everyone can be humble. Actually, it is the life lived between man and God, where he feels he is nothing and that everything good in him is from God and without God he is only dust.

St Isaac the Syrian says: "Whoever remembers his sins in order to be humble, is not actually being humble. Although this is good, he is only approaching humility. A true humble person does not need to convince himself or remind himself to feel humble but it becomes natural for him to consider himself as no one".

St John Climacus says: "A humble person is not the one who blames himself, for each one can tolerate self-criticism, but a really humble person is the one who can accept criticism from another and continue loving them."

Thus humility is not an easy virtue. It needs us to crush our wishes and our bodily desires. Our Lord taught us, "Whoever wants to be first, should be last." One should always look at Jesus' amazing humility and learn from it, though we can never reach His level.

Humility is not an isolated virtue but it is the basis of

all virtues. We cannot obtain any other virtue without it.

Humility or self denial cannot be reached through reading spiritual books or listening to spiritual talks or even by communicating with the saints. It is a deep relationship with God and a continual effort, which then frees man from all sin.

It is the narrow door that those seeking the kingdom of God must enter. It is the Cross that the honest disciple carries, following the steps of His Master. Is there any narrower door or any heavier Cross than surrendering one's self?

It is an exam to those seeking God. Joshua, Son of Sirach says: "Gold is tried through fire and people are tried through humility." (Sir 2:5)

The saints understood this and expressed it through their experience.

St John Climacus says: "Some said it is forgetting all the good one has done. Others said it is when man considers himself the lowest and the most sinful. Others said it is the awareness of one's weakness and the controlling of one's wishes. I say it is a blessing that only those who have it know it. The Lord said: 'Learn from Me for I am gentle and lowly in heart.' Learn from the Lord, not from an angel or another man or a book, and 'you will find rest for your souls.'"

THE HONOR OF THE VIRTUE OF HUMILITY

If pride is the worst of sins and leads to many other sins, then humility is the first of virtues and it is the basis of all other virtues. So whoever masters humility, establishes a strong foundation for his spiritual life. The fathers compare it to the Tree of Life.

It is an honor, as the Lord Jesus Christ Himself taught it, through His life, behavior and spiritual teachings. He did not say "Learn from Me how to perform miracles, heal the sick and raise the dead" but said: "Learn from Me for I am gentle and lowly in heart" (Matt 11:29). St Peter says: "Let this mind be in you which was also in Christ Jesus, who, being in the form of God, did not consider it robbery to be equal with God, but made Himself of no reputation, taking the form of a bondservant, and coming in the likeness of men." (Phil 2:7-9) St Pachomius says: "If you see a humble pure man, you have seen a great sight, for you have seen God through him." A monk once said to St Timothy the Hermit: "I always see my mind with God." The saint replied: "Better to see yourself below everyone, for there is no failure with humility."

St Augustine says: "Humility attracts God to you, though He is Almighty, but if you are conceited, He will withdraw." He also says: "Pride expelled angels from heaven while humility made God descend from heaven to earth. It threw Adam from Paradise while humility permitted the thief to enter Paradise. It drowned Pharaoh in the Red Sea while humility saved Moses."

The honor of this virtue is related to its place among other virtues. One asked St Macarius the Great: "Which is the greatest virtue?" He replied: "If haughtiness is the worst evil as it expelled angels from heaven, then no doubt humility is the greatest as it can raise sinners from the pit of sin."

Humility

We can obtain heavenly gifts through our humility. St John Climacus says: "If you heard about someone who can perform miracles, then be assured that he reached that through his humility." St Isaac says: "Talents are not given as a result of works but for the humility when these works are performed."

Humility is an honor because God loves modest people. The Psalmist says: "Though the LORD is on high, yet He regards the lowly" (Psalm 138:6). He lives with them: "For thus says the High and Lofty One Who inhabits eternity, whose name is Holy: "I dwell in the high and holy place, with him who has a contrite and humble spirit, to revive the spirit of the humble, and to revive the heart of the contrite ones." (Is 57:15)

Humility is the holy attire that the saints wear (1 Peter 5:5) and walk in. (Eph 4:1-2) St Paul says: "Therefore, as the elect of God, holy and beloved, put on tender mercies, kindness, humility, meekness and longsuffering." (Col 3:12)

Humble people have a special place in heaven. The Lord says: "Therefore whoever humbles himself as this little child is the greatest in the kingdom of heaven." (Matt 18:4)

Lastly, it is the Christian virtue that scientists and philosophers of the world could not learn or practice. Plato, the philosopher, prepared a banquet and invited some philosophers who were known to live a simple life. Philosopher Diognus was with them. Plato had decorated his house with precious carpets and tapestries. Diognus entered with filthy shoes and dirty clothes and stepped over those precious carpets. When Plato asked him what he was doing, he replied "I am stepping on the haughtiness and pride of Aphlatone." Plato replied saying: "Yes, you are stepping on the pride of Plato but you are doing this with another kind of pride!"

HUMILITY IN THE LORD'S LIFE AND THE LIVES OF HIS SAINTS

HUMILITY IN THE LIFE OF THE LORD JESUS CHRIST

Humility is the amazing robe that the Almighty God wore to show us Himself. It was impossible for the dust to see the Lord of Lords in His Divinity. When He used to show His Glory on Mount Sinai, the mountain trembled, "And so terrifying was the sight that Moses said, "I am exceedingly afraid and trembling." (Heb 12:18-21)

In the Old Testament, people could not approach the mountain when Your Glory ascended, while in the New Testament, the age of Grace and Humility, Your mother held You and Simon the Elder carried You in his arms (Luke 2:28). You ate and drank with humans and then gave us Yourself.

It was impossible for mankind to see the Son of God except in the robe of humility. "But You are holy, enthroned in the praises of Israel" (Psalm 22:3) Thus St Augustine compared the Lord's Humanity with humility. He said that the Son of God became human to reconcile mankind with God and to cure the human heart from pride. He accomplished the first with His Death and the second with His humility. Thus the life of the Lord Jesus Christ was full of love, humility and pain.

St Basil the Great recalled the life of Jesus Christ from His birth to His death and concluded that the Lord Jesus taught us the virtue of humility throughout all His life. In humility, the Lord shared our nature, "but made Himself of no reputation, taking the form of a bondservant, and coming in the likeness of men." (Phil 2:7). He showed humility in His birth, being born from a poor mother, in a lowly place as though he was the poorest in the world. He showed humility by escaping from Herod, as if He was the weak one, while in fact, He is the support of all weak people. He also obeyed His Mother, St Mary, and His father, Joseph the Carpenter (Luke 2:51). He came to John the Baptist to be baptised as though a sinner. He lived a poor life, out of His will and by His choice: "For you know the grace of Our Lord Jesus Christ, that though He was rich, yet for your sakes He became poor, that you through His poverty might become rich." (2 Cor 8:9) He accepted many insults from the Pharisees and chief priests and accepted death on the Cross. (Psalm 22:6; 69:9; Is 52:3). The Apostle expressed this saying: "And being found in appearance as a man, He humbled Himself and became obedient to the point of death, even the death of the cross." (Phil 2:8)

St Augustine and St Ironimos noticed that the Lord Jesus started his Sermon on the Mountain with the topic of Humility saying "Blessed are the poor in the spirit." The Lord lived this humble life although it ended in His Death.

Christ said: "Foxes have holes and birds of the air have nests, but the Son of Man has nowhere to lay His head."(Matt 8:20). He revealed His Glory on the Transfiguration Mountain to only three of His Disciples yet revealed His Death to many nations. On His Cross, the sign was written in the three major languages of the world.

Moreover, He asked these three disciples not to disclose what they saw to anyone until after His Resurrection (Matt 17:9). When the multitude wanted Him to be their King, He disappeared (John 6:15). When they wanted to insult Him, He gave Himself willingly.

The first sin that caused the fall of mankind was pride and it is no wonder that God counteracted it with humility. Probably the most prominent thing that the Lord did was when He knelt down and washed the disciples' feet (John 12:3-5). At first, St John recorded the Divinity of the Saviour saying "Jesus, knowing that the Father had given all things into His hands, and that He had come from God and was going to God," Then, he recounted His amazing humility: " ... rose from supper and laid aside His garments, took a towel and girded Himself. After that, He poured water into a basin and began to wash the disciples' feet, and to wipe them with the towel with which He was girded." Taking off clothes is a sign of taking off one's personal pride and glory. Washing the feet indicates great humility, humble service and care.

After finishing, the Lord explained the spiritual commandment: "Do you know what I have done to you? You call Me Teacher and Lord, and you say well, for so I am. If I then, your Lord and Teacher, have washed your feet, you also ought to wash one another's feet. For I have given you an example, that you should do as I have done to you. Most assuredly, I say to you, a servant is not greater than his master; nor is he who is sent greater than he who sent him. If you know these things, blessed are you if you do them" (John 13:12-17).

Humility in the Lives of the saints:

"If anyone desires to come after Me, let him deny himself, take up his cross, and follow Me." (Matt 16:24) "And whoever does not bear his cross and come after Me, cannot be My disciple." (Luke 14:27)

Self denial is the first criteria in Christian discipleship. The saints understood this fully and followed it. They struggled and denied themselves, remembering the Lord's Words: "A servant is not greater than his master" and thus they were glorified.

The saints understood that humility is the foundation for their spiritual life and struggled to acquire it. Mother Theodora, the nun, expressed this saying: "No asceticism, or effort or fasting can replace total humility."

A holy man who could cast out demons, once asked the demons: "What is it that can cast you out? Is it fasting?

Devil: We don't eat.

Monk: Is it staying awake in vigil?

Devil: We don't sleep

Monk: Is it leaving the world?

Devil: We live in deserted places.

Monk: So what casts you out then?

Devil: Nothing but humility.

It was said about St Anthony's struggle against the

Humility

devils that he used to tell them: "if you are strong, what do you want from a weak person like me? What will happen to me if you all gather against me? Don't you know that I am just dust and I cannot fight against your youngest?" He used to lie on the ground and scream saying: "Help me God for I am weak. Do not forsake me as I cannot fight any of them." When the devils heard this prayer, they ran away and could not hurt him because of His humility.

The saints were Spiritual giants but felt they were the worst sinners. Thus their life was full of tears. They did not force themselves to cry, but they felt this way when they realized the Majesty of God and His humility and Love. Abraham said about himself: "Indeed now, I who am but dust and ashes, have taken it upon myself to speak to the Lord." (Gen 18:27). When John the Baptist was asked about himself, he said: "I am the voice of one crying in the wilderness, Make straight the way of the Lord" (John 1:23). St Paul thought of himself as the worst in the world (1 Cor 14:23), and even called himself the first of the sinners (1 Tim 1:15). As a result, their self denial lifted them in the sight of God. The saints are like a tree full of fruit, whose branches lean towards the earth, contrary to branches without fruits, which will stand high. They are like burnt coal hidden under ashes, but this does not prevent their heat from warming anyone who comes close to it.

The saints in their humility continued struggling and never stopped. While in the flesh, they always aimed at higher spirituality. One of the saints gave this advice to his disciple: "If your thoughts praise you, ask them, why are you praising me? Travelers in sea are never confident, even if the sea is calm, because they can expect any storm. Many were near the port but were lost."

Although these saints reached high spiritual levels, they always attributed any talents to the power of God. St Macarius the Great once talked to a dead man and he answered him. When his disciples were astonished, he said: "This incident did not happen for me, for I am nothing. God did it for the sake of the dead man's widow and children."

The saints were careful to hide any virtues and if they were compelled to mention a miracle as a teaching to their disciples, they would never relate it to themselves, but to others.

Their humble behaviour led them to a high spiritual level. They called it "death to the world." They lived as though dead from the world but alive in Jesus Christ, accepting any hardships or insults. St Macarius the Great wanted to teach a brother a lesson. He told him to go to the cemetery and curse the dead. This brother went, cursed and stoned the dead. The saint then asked: "Did the dead answer you at all?" The brother said: "No." So the saint said: "Then, tomorrow go and praise them." The brother went and stood in the cemetery and said: "You are holy and pure." When he returned, the saint asked again: "Did they answer you?" He said: "No." So the saint said: "If you truly died with Christ and was buried with Him, you do like those who are dead, for a dead person is not affected by any praise or insult, and thus you can be saved."

HUMILITY IS THE FOUNDATION OF ALL VIRTUES

The saints agree that Humility is the foundation of all virtues. St Cyprian called it "The basis of holiness." St Jerome called it "The first Christian virtue." They compare it to the root of a tree, for a tree cannot grow higher or bear fruit unless its root is deep in the earth. They also compare it to the foundation of a house. The size of the foundation will affect the size of the building, just like humility, which is the basis of our spiritual life.

Father John Cassian says: "As a principle in the spiritual conduct of the early monastic fathers, it is impossible to attain purity of heart or any other virtue without attributing it to God because that is real humility. Thus the saints considered it the foundation of all virtues."

It is not only the foundation of all virtues but it is the support of all virtues and with it comes God's help. St Isaac mentions: "Remember that your purity and virtue is not because of your careful life but it is God's Grace that carries you. If you start thinking in a proud manner, then cry and be sorrowful until you are saved from this thought. Acquire humility and your sins will be forgiven. Many sins can be defeated by humility." St Isaac mentions that God lifts up those with humble minds. A humble mind saves from many sins because many of Satan's battles are a result of pride.

But is there a contradiction in saying that humility is the foundation of all virtues while faith is the basis?

No, there is no contradiction. The foundation of a house depends on two things: digging and getting the dirt out of the rocky land, before laying the foundation. It is Humility which digs deep to the Rock, that is Jesus Christ. (1 Cor 10:4) You dig the land with humility, remove all dirt (which is self-dependence) and then the foundation (which is faith) will be firm.

HUMILITY IS THE FOUNDATION OF MANY VIRTUES SUCH AS:

1) Faith needs humility because a proud mind cannot easily accept faith. The Lord Jesus says: "How can you believe, who receive honor from one another," (John 5:44). Humility is also necessary to maintain faith as many heresies were the result of pride. St Paul says: "But know this, that in the last days perilous times will come: For men will be ... boasters, proud, blasphemers. "(2 Tim 3:1-2)

2) Hope needs humility as a support, for man hopes only what he can see but he needs to hope for what he cannot see. The person who depends on his knowledge will not accept what he cannot see. Hoping in unseen matters requires a humble mind.

3) Love and humility co-exist and sustain each other. St John Climacus says: "Nothing is better than love and humility for humility lifts up and love never fails." Love refers to our love to God and our love for each other.

Our love of God is strengthened by humility. When one feels the burden of his sins but also feels the steadfastness of the Lord's Love, the feeling of humility helps to keep the love of God in the heart. These feelings moved many saints to the love of God. For example, St Mary in the magnificat: "My soul magnifies the Lord, and my spirit has rejoiced in God my Savior, for He has regarded the lowly state of His maidservant." (Luke 1:47)

As for our love for each other, this needs a lot of humility. Blaming others, envy and anger are all a result of pride. A humble person does not get upset if no one gives him a compliment or if another person was praised instead of himself. He will love it when good things happen to other people and will feel that they deserve praise more than himself. St John the Baptist says: "He must increase, but I must decrease." (John 3:30). St Paul mentions: "being of one accord, of one mind. In lowliness of mind let each esteem others better than himself." (Phil 2:2-3). Also St John says:"By this we know love, because He laid down His life for us. And we also ought to lay down our lives for the brethren." (1 John 3:16)

People usually dislike a proud person because he never admits his mistake. He does not obey others and will not pardon because he does not want to appear weak. He has a temper and only believes in his opinion. A humble person is the opposite and is loved by everyone.

If we contemplate God's love for us, how He gave Himself for us and how he bore all insults and sufferings, we will be led into humility.

4) Prayer is unacceptable if it is offered without humility. Jesus son of Sirach says: "A humble prayer penetrates the clouds and continues until the Almighty hears it." (Sir 32:17) The humble Judith cried to the Lord while in sackcloth saying: "You refused the proud from

the beginning and always accepted the supplications of the humble." (Judith 9:11). The Lord accepted the prayer of the tax collector and commended him (Luke 18: 13,14).

5) Humility relates to other virtues like obedience, chastity, etc... Sometimes falling in adultery is a result of a proud heart. Only through humility and supplication to God is this temptation lifted.

What Does Humility Do?

It has many blessings and the Lord bestows His Grace where humility exists. St Ephraim the Syrian says: "Whoever wants to move a rock from its place will put something underneath to lift it and then it can be rolled easily. This is humility."

Its blessings can be shown in the following aspects:

It restores man to his original status:

Man's first sin was pride, so humility will definitely restore him to his first status through God's humility in taking our Humanity. Pride expelled the first man from paradise and humility can return him.

St Anthony asked his disciples: "My sons, why did Jesus Christ wash the feet of disciples, Himself? It was to teach us humility. All those who want to return to their first status cannot do so except through humility."

Casting Out demons:

The proud devil was deprived from his status due to his pride and so he cannot face a humble person. Humility makes him disappear!

This is a fact experienced by saints in their spiritual struggle. Saints saw this in visions or heard it from the demons while exorcising them.

It was said about St Anthony that he once saw the devil's net spread all over the world and he sighed saying: "Lord who can escape from this?" So he heard a voice from heaven saying: "The humble ones can escape."

Also, it was told about St Macarius the Great that the devil met him once and told him: "Woe to you Macarius for whatever you do I do also. You fast, and I don't eat. You stay awake, and I don't sleep, but one thing you defeat me with." The saint asked: "What is that?" The devil answered: "You defeat me with humility alone."

An elderly monk said: "If a monk forgave his brother in a humble way, the demons are burnt." In the paradise of the desert fathers, a strange story confirms this:

There were two monks living together in a holy loving manner. The devil wanted to separate them. One night the younger monk lit a lamp and put it on a lamp stand and the devil made it fall down and its light went off. The elder monk was angry and hit the younger monk. But this young monk knelt down and said: "Please don't be upset and be patient with me and I will light it again." Then this devil went and told the leader of the devils what happened. A priest of idols heard this incident and saw how the devil burnt as a result of the humility of this young monk. The priest of idols immediately left everything, believed and became a monk. He practiced total humility and always said that humility defeats Satan and all his powers.

IT PRESERVES THE GRACE OF GOD IN MAN:

It provides the right environment for other virtues to grow and develop. If a man boasts about his virtues he will lose them. Just like the ashes preserve the heat of the burnt coal and cover it so that one thinks it is not burning, humility will also preserve our spiritual virtues.

HUMILITY LIFTS UP THE HUMBLE:

St Peter says: "Be clothed with humility, for God resists the proud, But gives grace to the humble. Therefore humble yourselves under the mighty hand of God, that He may exalt you in due time." (1 Peter 5: 5-6).

James the Apostle says: "Humble yourselves in the sight of the Lord, and He will lift you up." (James 4:10).

In the book of Isaiah Isaiah, the Lord says: "But on this one will I look: On him who is poor and of a contrite spirit, and who trembles at My word." (Is 66:2).

St John Climacus says: "If the devil has fallen from heaven because of pride, then humility can lift man back up to heaven."

The Lord says "Whoever exalts himself will be humbled and he who humbles himself will be exalted."

The Lord also praised the Centurion who felt unworthy to accept Jesus inside his house: "I have not found such great faith, not even in Israel!" (Matt 8:10).

Furthermore, the Pharisee who prayed in the temple with pride, was refused: "I am not like other men—extortioners, unjust, adulterers, or even as this tax collector. I fast twice a week; I give tithes of all that I possess." However, the tax collector who prayed humbly, found more favour with God: "Lord have mercy upon me for I am a sinner." (Luke 18:9-14).

John the Baptist felt unworthy to untie the sandal straps of Jesus, yet he became His beloved and this unworthy hand became worthy to be placed upon the head of Christ in Baptism at the Jordan River: "Permit it to be so now, for thus it is fitting for us to fulfill all righteousness." (Matt 3:15)

Hannah, Samuel's mother says: "He raises the poor from the dust and lifts the beggar from the ash heap, to set them among princes and make them inherit the throne of glory." (1 Sam 2:8). David the prophet says the same in Psalm 113. St Mary mentioned: "He has shown strength with His arm; He has scattered the proud in the imagination of their hearts. He has put down the mighty from their thrones, and exalted the lowly. He has filled the hungry with good things, and the rich He has sent away empty." (Luke 1:51-53)

The Lord Jesus Himself, "humbled Himself...Therefore God also has highly exalted Him and given Him the name which is above every name, that at the name of Jesus every knee should bow, of those in heaven, and of those on earth, and of those under the earth." (Phi 2:7-10)

SECRETS ARE REVEALED AND TALENTS GIVEN:

David the prophet says: "The secret of the LORD is with those who fear Him," (Psalm 25:14). Solomon says that God's secret is with the upright (Proverbs 3:32), and none is more upright than the humble. The Lord Jesus Christ, after rebuking Capernaum for its pride said: "Thank You, Father, Lord of heaven and earth, that You have hidden these things from the wise and prudent and have revealed them to babes. Even so, Father, for so it seemed good in Your sight." (Matt 11: 23-26). The children here are the humble.

St Isaac says: "Talents are not given for works but for the spirit of humility that the works are done with." He also says: "From sadness comes humility and by humility talents are given. Consequently, talents are not given because of one's works but as a result of humility." He also says: "Before falling is pride, and before talents are humility."

ITS FRUIT IS JOY AND PEACE IN THE HEART:

One of the fruits of humility is the inner peace and the joy that cannot be described. The Lord says: "Learn from Me, for I am gentle and lowly in heart, and you will find rest for your souls." (Matt 11:29). David the Prophet says: "My soul shall make its boast in the LORD; the humble shall hear of it and be glad." (Psalm 34:2). Also: "You have turned for me my mourning into dancing; You have put off my sackcloth and clothed me with gladness." (Psalm 30:11). St Pachomius says: "Be humble to become joyful, for joy accompanies humility."

Anxiety and trouble affect the proud. For example, Haman was upset when Mordecai did not give him the respect he wanted (Esther 5:9).

THE HUMBLE ARE WISE:

Solomon the wise man says: "When pride comes, then comes shame; but with the humble is wisdom."

(Proverb 11:2). Also about wisdom: "Wisdom is good with an inheritance, and profitable to those who see the sun." (Eccles 7:11). David the Prophet mentions: "The testimony of the LORD is sure, making wise the simple." (Ps 19:7). Jesus Son of Sirach says: "The wisdom of the humble raises him up and seats him among the great." (Sir 11:1).

St John Climacus says: "Meekness is the key to knowledge, for God teaches the humble His ways." St Ephram the Syrian mentions: "The wise spirit lies in the meek and humble." St Pachomius says: "Be humble so that the Lord can protect you and strengthen you." For the Lord looks at the humble and it is written that "He leads the meek and teaches the humble His ways."

IT PROVIDES PATIENCE AND TOLERANCE:

A proud man is constantly complaining and feeling disadvantaged, while people are against him. Unlike the humble person who knows his shortcomings and bears whatever comes his way. The humble blames himself for everything and does not care much about what people think of him. His aim is only to do God's will, as Micah the prophet says: "Therefore I will look to the LORD; I will wait for the God of my salvation; …I will bear the indignation of the LORD, because I have sinned against Him." (Micah 7,9). Consequently, humility trains us to be patient and tolerant. Jesus Son of Sirach says: "My son, if you come forward to serve the Lord, prepare yourself for trials. Have a humble heart and accept it. Stay close to God and be patient. Whatever happens, tolerate the pain and in your humility be patient." (Sir 2:1-4)

Humility

IT HELPS AND RELIEVES FROM HARDSHIPS:

We saw how humility trains us to be patient and tolerant. Patience and tolerance also help us in trials and hardships, whether the trial is to examine us, make us worthy or strengthen our wellbeing. St Paul says: "Nevertheless God, who comforts the downcast, comforted us." (2 Cor 7:6)

St Isaac says: "God permits trials, even for saints, so we continue to be humble. If we harden our hearts, God will allow harder temptations. But if we face these trials with a humble heart, God will be merciful." He also says: "Grace will test a man's heart, and will leave it to face temptations alone if it is self centered or conceited."

An elder once said: "Humility saved many without any pain, while the agony of man will be useless without humility. For many worked hard and were proud so were not saved."

In the battle of lust and adultery, humility is a major factor in lifting this war. St Augustine says: "We can only obtain purity when we realise that we cannot reach it by our own effort."

The Wiseman says: "When I realised that I could not be pure unless God made me, I went and pleaded to the Lord."

This is true as the historian Palladius wrote about St Palamon, an old man seventy years in age yet having to fight against thoughts of adultery for over 12 years. He was continually trying hard to conquer those thoughts but failed. He then heard a voice from heaven saying:

"The Lord allowed you this warfare so that you can acknowledge your weakness and poverty and stop relying on yourself. Humble yourself and depend only on the Lord in everything." St Palamon was consoled and the war was lifted from him.

Humility lifts the anger of God and it gives a response to prayer:

There are many examples in the Holy Bible such as what was told about Hezekiah, King of Judah: "Then Hezekiah humbled himself for the pride of his heart, he and the inhabitants of Jerusalem, so that the wrath of the LORD did not come upon them in the days of Hezekiah." (2 Chron 32:26) Similarly, Manasseh, King of Judah, did evil in the sight of the Lord so the soldiers of the king of Assyria took him with hooks and bound him with bronze fetters. "Now when he was in affliction, he implored the LORD his God, and humbled himself greatly before the God of his fathers, and prayed to Him; and He received his entreaty, heard his supplication, and brought him back to Jerusalem into his kingdom. (2 Chron 33:12).

Job also talked to God at the end of his trial saying: "I know that You can do everything, and that no purpose of Yours can be withheld from You. You asked, 'Who is this who hides counsel without knowledge? Therefore I have uttered what I did not understand, things too wonderful for me, which I did not know. Listen, please, and let me speak; You said, 'I will question you, and you shall answer Me.' I have heard of You by the hearing of the ear, but now my eye sees You. Therefore I abhor myself, and repent in dust and ashes." (Job 42:1-6). The Lord blessed the end of

Job and it was better than his beginning. (Job 42:9,10,12)

Nothing is stronger than the Lord's commandment to Solomon, the son of king David: "If My people who are called by My name will humble themselves, and pray and seek My face, and turn from their wicked ways, then I will hear from heaven, and will forgive their sin and heal their land." (2 Cor 7:14)

How can we obtain humility?

There are people who are humble by nature and there are those who obtained humility through spiritual struggle and much spiritual training. We do not deny that it is a difficult road but it is the same narrow road leading to the City of Joy. It is a long road and needs continuous training, subduing one's will and wishes. St John Climacus says: "In the beginning, we hate praise reluctantly then as humility increases through different virtues, a person reaches a stage where he considers himself unworthy. Similar to a plant that continues to grow as long as it is watered."

We will discuss some issues that will help us obtain this virtue:

First : Imitate the humility of our Saviour:

There are many verses from the Bible which tells us to imitate Christ's humility. The Apostle says: "Looking unto Jesus, the author and finisher of our faith" (Heb 12:2), and "Imitate me, just as I also imitate Christ" (1 Cor 11:1).

The first of these blessings is meekness and humility as the Lord invited us, "Learn from Me, for I am gentle and lowly in heart" (Matt 11:29).

St John Climacus says: "The Lord said learn from me for I am gentle and lowly in heart. Not to learn from an angel, another person, or a book, but from Me."

St Ephram the Syrian says: "What can we say to God? What did we ever need and He did not supply? Haven't we seen God humble Himself as a slave so that we too become humble? Haven't we seen His Holy Face spitted on so that if someone scolded us we don't reply? Haven't we seen His back bend from beatings so that we submit to our superiors? And His face slapped so we do not respond when rejected. We did not hear him arguing so that we do not stick to our opinion and do not answer back? We heard Him saying I do nothing from My own, so that we do not become important in our own eyes. We even heard Him say, 'Learn from me for I am gentle and lowly in heart.'

Second: Know yourself:

The saints always denied themselves because they saw themselves in God's light. Just like dust cannot be seen in a dark room, without sunlight. We do not discover some of our sins except through God's light. One of the fathers said: "When one knows himself, then he is on the way to know God." Just like the old philosophy 'Know yourself because once you do, you will be humble.'

Humility is not learned from books or from lectures but is learnt from real knowledge of oneself. St Isaac says:

"Blessed is the man who knows his weakness. For this knowledge will lead him to control himself from laziness and ask for God's help and depend on Him." To reach this knowledge, we need to contemplate a few points:

<u>Contemplate on your real self:</u>

God made us free and we were saved freely also, "and were by nature children of wrath" (Eph 2:3). The Lord Himself called us from darkness to His great light (1 Peter 2:9) so we became His beloved sons and daughters. This was not because of our worthiness but because of His mercy. He is still supporting us and guiding us so we do not fall.

Who am I really? I am nothing but dust. God created me from dust and is keeping me and protecting me. David the prophet says: "You have hedged me behind and before, and laid Your hand upon me." (Psalm 139:5). So if the Lord left me for a second, I will return to nothing. The Apostle explained this saying: "For what is your life? It is even a vapor that appears for a little time and then vanishes away." (James 4:14)

The beauty of man; his mind, strength, wisdom and capacity are all from God. Man himself will return to dust in spite of all the advances in science. He is from dust and will return to dust, and the spirit will return to God who created it. (Eccl 12:7). Job realised this when he said: "say to corruption, 'You are my father', and to the worm, You are my mother and my sister." (Job 17:14)

This truth was discovered by the early saints. Jacob said to God: "I am not worthy of the least of all the mercies and of all the truth which You have shown Your servant;

for I crossed over this Jordan with my staff, and now I have become two companies." (Gen 32:10).

Moses knew his weakness: "Who am I that I should go to Pharaoh, and that I should bring the children of Israel out of Egypt?" (Ex 3:11), and also "O my Lord, I am not eloquent, neither before nor since You have spoken to Your servant; but I am slow of speech and slow of tongue." (Ex 4:10).

David in his final prayer said: "But who am I, and who are my people, that we should be able to offer so willingly as this? For all things come from You, and of Your own we have given You. For we are aliens and pilgrims before You, as were all our fathers; our days on earth are as a shadow, and without hope. O LORD our God, all this abundance that we have prepared to build You a house for Your Holy Name is from Your hand, and is all Your own." (1 Chron 29:14-16).

St Isaac says: "Do not depend on your strength so you are not left to your weakness. You will realise it when you fall. Remember that any matter that a man boasts about may be changed by the Lord so that this person becomes humble."

<u>Think about your sins:</u>

To know yourself is to know your sins and weaknesses. St Augustine prayed saying: "Lord, let me understand myself and know You." To reach this knowledge, we should evaluate ourselves on the standard of the Holy Bible. It is the lamp that lights the way to heaven (Psalm 119:105). It was written for us (Rom 15:4). We are required to learn all commandments to reach the perfection of Christian life. (Matt 5:48) We are required to lead a life of holiness "without which no one will see the Lord." (Heb 12:14).

Compare yourself with those better, like the saints. We should remember "Now If the righteous one is scarcely saved, Where will the ungodly and the sinner appear?" It is important to communicate with spiritual people in order to learn from them but also have quiet time with yourself to check your behaviour and progress.

Realise the changes in yourself:

It is important to realise that people change. You should never be confident in yourself, even if you have acquired a few virtues. St Moses the Black says: "Do not trust yourself while you are still alive."

Before the departure of St Shishawy, a sick elderly father from Upper Egypt, the monks gathered around him. They heard him talking as if to a crowd but they did not see anyone. The monks asked him "What are you seeing father?" He said, "There is a crowd coming to take my spirit and I am asking them to wait for a while so that I may repent." One of the monks asked: "Even if they left you for a while, can you succeed in repenting while you are that old?" The saint replied: "I cannot do anything now but I can just sigh and weep." One of the monks said: "Your repentance is complete now." But the saint said: "Believe me, I do not know of I have started at all." Then his face shone and he uttered his last words: "Look, here is the Lord saying get this repentant man of the desert." The room was filled with sweet fragrance and he passed away.

<u>Rejoice when insulted:</u>

A man gradually grows in his spiritual life and in all virtues. Humility grows with practice and effort. Initially when a person is insulted, he is upset and even may respond with anger. Soon, he can control himself and control his feelings. Instead of feeling upset, he remains peaceful. Ultimately he feels glad, just like the disciples when they were beaten for preaching the Word of God "they departed from the presence of the council, rejoicing that they were counted worthy to suffer shame for His name." (Act 5:41)

There is a higher level than this: A person will not only rejoice when insulted but will reach out to it. There was a struggling monk who lived in the desert but travelled to the monastery in Upper Egypt. All the monks in this monastery were holy. After spending a few days, he asked the Abbot to permit him to leave. When the Abbot asked him for the reason, he said: "There is no suffering here. All the fathers are saints and I am a sinner. I need to go where I am insulted and cursed, for by this manner a sinner will be saved." The Abbot was amazed and allowed him to leave saying: "Go and be strong."

We should be patient if insulted and even rejoice, knowing that it will save us from false glory and will keep us humble. St Paul says: "I take pleasure in infirmities, in reproaches" (2 Cor 12:10)

THIRD : DO NOT BOAST ABOUT SPIRITUAL TALENTS:

This level of humility is more superior to the above. It is no surprise if a sick man feels his sickness or the poor his poverty or the sinner his sins, but it is strange when a rich man considers himself poor or if an honoured saint believes himself to be the worst sinner!

Saints with many talents repeat with the twenty four priests: "You are worthy, O Lord, to receive glory and honor and power; for You created all things, and by Your will they exist and were created." (Rev 4:11); or what St Paul said: "Not that we are sufficient of ourselves to think of anything as being from ourselves, but our sufficiency is from God." (2 Cor 3:5) "For it is God who works in you both to will and to do for His good pleasure." (Php 2:13). They believe that any good thing is from God, "Every good gift and every perfect gift is from above, and comes down from the Father of lights." (James 1:17). They feel that their life and spiritual growth is derived from Jesus, "As the branch cannot bear fruit of itself, unless it abides in the vine, neither can you, unless you abide in Me." (John 15:4). Consequently, they contribute all their talents to God.

When the disciples rejoiced that the demons obeyed them, Jesus warned them saying: "Nevertheless do not rejoice in this... I saw Satan fall like lightning from heaven." (Luke 10: 18, 20) We need God's support to maintain humility while acquiring spiritual talents. St Ambrose says: "No one can do this from himself, only through the great Grace of God."

The Apostle says: "Now we have received, not the spirit of the world, but the Spirit who is from God, that we might know the things that have been freely given to us by God." (1 Cor 2:12)

John Cassian also says: "Just like the eye cannot see on its own, except with the assistance of light, a person cannot do good on his own, even if he is righteous, except with the assistance of the Grace of God."

"Unless the LORD guards the city, the watchman stays awake in vain." (Psalm 127: 1)

Practicing humility

We can practice humility through: simple clothing, leaving out accessories whether in clothing, food or drink; serving others, doing chores that others feel degrading; obeying superiors and elders based on real love and humility; and apologizing quickly after any mistake.

These practices have a huge impact on acquiring real humility because any virtue is obtained through practice and any outer action causes inner change. Our Lord Jesus Himself taught us humility in a practical way; He lowered Himself, washed the disciples' feet and commanded them to do the same.

St Basil the Great says: "Science and trades cannot be mastered without practice. So whoever wants to master philosophy, poetry, or any trade must continuously practice it. Similarly, humility and other virtues can only be mastered through practice."

St Augustine says: "The outer person and his inner self are linked to each other so whenever the body acts in a humble way the heart also reacts in a similar way. So if you bowed and accepted to kiss your brother's feet, your heart will react in a humble way as well. Any outer action done in a humble manner affects the heart."

General advice:

- Do not say things in front of others that may result in them praising you. Sometimes people say negative things about themselves so that others admire them.

- If people praise you for something good, immediately give thanks to God, who helped you accomplish this matter. If you think highly of yourself, remember your hidden sins that others are not aware of and you will feel that you are not worthy to be praised.

- Do not perform anything that will cause people to praise you. The Lord says: "Take heed that you do not do your charitable deeds before men, to be seen by them. Otherwise you have no reward from your Father in heaven." (Matt 6:1). Whatever you do, do for the Lord who will reward you.

- Do not excuse yourself. "Do not incline my heart to any evil thing, to practice wicked works." (Psalm 141:4) Be frank with yourself and honest in your evaluation. Be quick to apologise to God and to others.

- Consider everyone better than yourself. "Let nothing be done through selfish ambition or conceit, but in lowliness of mind let each esteem others better than himself." (Phil 2:3)

- Do not adore high places and centres of attention. The Lord cursed the Pharisees for this. (Matt 23:6)

- Do not be quick to talk in any gathering. If possible be the last to talk, feeling that others are better than you. St Pachomius says: "Be humble in everything, and if you know all wisdom, then be the last to talk."

- Do not allow yourself to day dream about great positions even if it appears to be for the glory of God and spreading His Word. For example, do not imagine yourself a Bishop who plans for the welfare of the Church and makes major reforms. Beware of this for the devil of pride is hiding behind these thoughts.

Some aids to Humility

Deeds of Repentance:

These generally help us to be humble. Though humility is the basis of all virtues, it is also nourished by them.

St John Climacus says: "There is a relationship between repentance, tears and humility. The soul is refined like flour by repentance, then it is kneaded by tears like dough then it is cooked like bread by the fire of humility which is a gift from God."

The prophet mentions: "I was humble so please save me." He also says: "Repentance awakens man, tears knock on the door of heaven, and a humble mind opens the door of the Kingdom."

Feeling like a Stranger:

St John Climacus says: "The feeling of being an absolute foreigner results in humility." A person who feels like a stranger in this world does not care if people know him or if they praise him. Being a stranger gives us a feeling of being "dead from the world" which strongly helps us remain humble. The person who feels like a stranger, looks forward to the eternal life and repeats with

the Psalmist: "Woe to me, I am a stranger for long."
The Lord gives special assistance to the stranger as the Psalmist says: "The LORD watches over the strangers." (Psalm 147:9) St Paul says: "Therefore God is not ashamed to be called their God." (Heb 11:16)

Tolerating hardships with patience:

This also keeps us humble. St Isaac says: "God allows temptations and hardships for the righteous so that they realise their weakness, for hardships result in humility. He may permit them to suffer from natural causes or from other people's actions or sometimes from poverty, sickness or need. They may even suffer from bad thoughts. All of these will help them acknowledge their weakness and keep humble."

Regarding His people, the Lord says: "I also have walked contrary to them and have brought them into the land of their enemies" (Lev 26:41).

St Isaac says: "It is true God, You do not stop from subjecting us to various trials until we become humble." He also says: "Through temptations, we approach humility and those who do not suffer any sorrows or temptations, the door of pride and haughtiness is open before them."

Leaving Everything:

The love of ownership in its various appearances makes a person more attached to the world. Instead, not attaching one's self to anything of the world relieves us to live a free spirit. Our worldly life weakens our spirit. The spirit which the Lord blessed in the beginning of the Sermon on the Mount (Matt 5:3). That is why the saintly fathers advise us to live a poor life full of humility.

St Isaac says: "A person who is worried about material things of the world or is attached to any of it, cannot be humble nor have a pure heart, for a humble person is dead to the world and the world is dead to him and he cannot love anything in it. So if you want to be humble, release yourself first from worldly matters and follow God in hope, faith and love to gain a life that is eternal."

Practical aspects of Humility

We will talk about the practical aspects of Humility and not just the theoretical side. We will mention only a few practices and you, my brother, should measure the other aspects of your life accordingly:

In Prayer:

Many times we feel proud when we regularly practice certain spiritual exercises. For example when one prays regularly, he may feel that he is becoming a saint, even more if the Lord allows him to shed a few tears in prayer. Thus prayer becomes a source of pride rather than blessing. Do not be proud of your prayers, my brother, for it cannot be compared to the prayer of our Lord who spent all night praying in Gethsemane. It cannot be compared to the prayers of saints whose lives were continual prayer.

Where are you compared to the great St Arsanious who used to stand for prayer every Sunday from sunset to sunrise the following day. He would spend the whole night in dialogue with God and feel upset when the night was over. Where are you compared to St Bishoy who used to tie his hair with a cord to the ceiling of his cell so that he can stay awake all night and fight the natural desire to sleep? Where are you compared to St Maximos and St Domadios, the sons of a Roman Emperor? The prayer of one appeared as a pillar of light extending from his mouth to heaven, while the prayer of the other appeared as fire from his mouth? This was seen by St Macarius the Great.

Where are you compared to St St Tegi (St Reweis) who sat contemplating the phrase "Our Father who art in heaven" for eight hours? Where are you compared to Elijah, the prophet, who prayed earnestly that it would not rain; and it did not rain on the land for three years and six months? (James 5:17)

Prayer in fact, is not just time spent standing before God, but it is life as a whole just as David said, "But I give myself to prayer." (Psalm 109:4) The Lord commanded us to pray always and without ceasing (1 Thes 5:17). So are you like that in your prayers?

What about prayer with faith, prayer by the spirit and mind? (1 Cor 14:15) What about prayer of thanksgiving and the other aspects of prayer that should be offered before God? (Col 4:2)

Even if you have fulfilled all these conditions, is there a reason for being proud in your prayer? You are a useless servant on your own for you did not stand for prayer without the Spirit of God moving you. The Apostle writes: "For we do not know what we should pray for as we ought, but the Spirit Himself makes intercession for us with groanings which cannot be uttered." (Rom 8:26) The thought of prayer is not your own, but of God. The words are from Him, even the expression of love is from God too. For everything is "from Him, of Him and Him in all things."

Therefore when you stand to pray, feel your worthlessness and ask your requests in a submissive way. For if we cautiously present our petitions to earthly rulers of this world hoping to receive our requests, should not we do the same when asking the Lord of Lords? Before prayer, you should spend a few moments in silence, remembering how lowly you are and how great God is in His love. During the time of prayer, He is allowing you to raise your voice and share with the angels in their praise. If you do so, you will feel God's blessing in prayer. A beggar does not wear expensive clothes and go out asking people for money because people will not give him. Similarly, present your poor self to God and He will have compassion on you.

IN FASTING:

In Christianity, prayer and fasting are not an obligation but we use them as weapons to conquer the devil as the Lord taught us: "This kind can come out by nothing but prayer and fasting." (Mark 9:29) Consequently, do not feel that you should be rewarded when you fast. You do not fast for God but for yourself, in order to conquer your body. It is not for your spiritual strength but for your weakness. Fasting is practiced in all religions but has no value if one does not fast from sin.

Your fasting cannot be compared to the fasting of the saints. Some saints defied human nature by fasting for very long periods, in order to draw closer to God. Where are you compared to Moses who fasted for 40 days or St Bishoy who used to fast 20 days at a time? Where are you compared to St Macarius of Alexandria who used to eat one boiled leaf of cabbage every Sunday during the forty days of fasting only so that his brothers would not stumble? Where are you compared to the many saints who would fast the whole forty days?

Even if you could do that, your fasting would not be accepted unless you refrain from sin and "Fast from every evil in purity."

In Charitable Deeds:

How do you feel when you are doing a charitable deed? When you give tithes do you feel that you have fulfilled your duty as ordered by God?

Regarding Quantity: Remember that giving tithes is just the minimal amount as mentioned in the Old Testament. As for the New Testament, the age of Grace, we are required to sell all that we have and give alms. (Luke 12:33) We are required to give generously (1 Tim 6:18) and give cheerfully. (2 Cor 9:7)

Regarding Quality: Give in self denial so you are rewarded by your heavenly Father who sees in secret. (Matt 6:1) Do not give in front of people for then you have received your reward.

The money that you give is not yours; it is God's and

God did not give you this money to keep you wealthy (Luke 12:21) but to keep you rich in good deeds. (1 Tim 6:18) You entered this world naked and will leave it naked too. So whenever you give and no matter how generously you give, it is only a part of your wealth. Others gave all they owned and even gave themselves to God.

St Anthony is an example of someone who gave all he owned to the poor. St Abraam, Bishop of Fayoum, was a living example of a merciful man in his generation. Ibrahim El Gohary was also a very merciful man. One day beggars decided to test him by repeatedly asking for help. One begger asked for aid eighteen times, during the same morning. Every time, Ibrahim El Gohary would give him money. The beggar was surprised and asked the saint why he was helping every single time. The saint replied: "What I have is a gift from my Lord Jesus Christ. How can I not return it when I am asked?" Even after he passed away, Ibrahim El Gohary supported a needy person, through a vision.

Pride

"God resists the proud, but gives grace to the humble."
(James 4: 6)

- The truth about pride
- What does pride do?
- Reasons leading to pride
- Pride in one's own eyes
- Characteristics of pride
- Pride disguised in virtues
- How can a person cure his pride?

My dear brethren, do not think that pride doesn't affect you but read carefully, dig into yourself and struggle to get rid of this sin as Jesus, Son of Sirach says, "for pride is the beginning of all sin: he that holds it, shall be filled with maledictions, and it shall ruin him in the end." (Sirach 10: 15)

Pride is when a person talks a lot about himself, falls in blasphemy, relates good deeds to himself or feels himself counted among the saints. If this is not the case, it doesn't mean you are free from this disease! You may be carrying the disease without feeling it. It is like cancer, you don't feel it at the beginning.

St John Cassian says, "Pride and vain glory start as minor pains, that's why it cannot be targeted quickly. All other pains are clear and can be fought if the soul is awake, pride is not so, one usually does not realise the war of pride easily. Pride and vain glory involve a harsher fight because they attack fiercely and interfere with all of our life's activities; like walking, talking, eating, keeping silent, in vigils and fastings, prayers, readings and hymns, long suffering, etc. The devil shoots arrows of pride and vain glory towards those who have acquired virtues, hoping to steal the reward of their struggle."

If you are trying hard to acquire virtues, don't think that this path will protect you from the disease, because it wages war against both: those who are walking in the path of virtues, and even more, those who are struggling to live a spiritual life. St. John of The Ladder, Abbot of Sinai Monasteries says, "The devil of despair rejoices with your numerous sins, while the devil of pride rejoices as you obtain numerous virtues."

St John Cassian also says, "The devil of pride is a cunning one, it attacks those who attained high spiritual levels in order to destroy the tower of their virtues. All diseases could be treated at their start, but this malignant disease, hits deeply and slowly to a far extent, thus its damage is huge and it severly breaks a person. It is well known that gluttony could be controlled by fasting, adultery by chastity, love of money by poverty, and anger by meekness. But the evil of pride becomes like an avenging leader who after surrounding a big city and conquering it, will demolish and ruin its foundations."

Pride is like a thief who sneaks into the bedroom and attacks his prey while it is sleeping or like a warrier who fights his enemy with a deadly blow or like the spy who is working on behalf of its enemies.

Thus, we should be aware of the devil's tricks and disclose his plans. We should deliver him to our King so that we do not become traitors to our Lord. For it is the Lord who truly owns us and reigns over our minds, hearts, bodies and lives.

Pride is a dangerous disease. In order to discover and remove it, one needs discernment and alertness.

In order to discover 'pride' early, you should answer the following questions:

Do you rejoice when someone praises you and get angry from those who rebuke or ridicule you?

Do you get more angry if the rebuke or instruction gets stronger?

Do you feel uncomfortable when someone speaks

about you?

How far is your obedience?

How far can you accept instructions and guidance from others?

How do you feel towards those whom you excel over, concerning knowledge, wisdom, virtue and richness? Do you feel sympathy and kindness towards them accompanied by thanksgiving to God Who granted you all these riches and enriched you with these virtues, or do you feel proud because you are much better?

Maybe now you are starting to change your personal view of yourself. Let's follow all the issues relating to this dangerous sin.

THE TRUTH ABOUT PRIDE

It is the Greatest and Most Dangerous Sin, in his book, "The Principles," Origan said "Someone might ask what is the greatest sin. It is well known that it is adultery or impurity or any other sin related to desire. It is true that these sins are awful and horrible, but they are not like the sin which the Holy Bible really denounces. Without a doubt, it is the sin of pride, haughtiness and self admiration. This is the sin of Satan and as a result, he fell from heaven to earth, because God resists the haughty ones."

It is the Mother of Many Other Sins, it is not a sin by itself like stealing or lying, but it is a mother, giving birth to other sins i.e. children of Satan. St. John of the Ladder says: "I tied this sin with the ropes of obedience and whipped it to tell me its secrets, so it answered, "I am the head and the mother of all other sins, nothing excels me, nothing contradicts me except humbleness and obedience. My children are: anger, envy, judging others, loud voice, arguments, blasphemy, and being convinced with your own opinion only. Vain glory is my ship, but meekness and self judgement mock the ship and its passengers."

It is a Shielding Tower for Many Other Sins, this is clear from St. John's words. For example, a proud person never says that he is wrong lest people should think he is a wrong doer. A proud person never apologizes lest they should think he is weak. He never obeys others lest they think his opinion is of less value than other opinions. He can never be meek or humble; he is always angry because he sticks to his rights and he always talks too much lest people think he is ignorant.

Pride is a stubborn opponent fighting us till the last breath, it doesn't follow a pattern in one's life, for example, the fight of desire gets stronger at youth, then calms down. Instead, pride never calms down. How many saints fell because of pride even after becoming hermits!! It is said about St. Macarius the Great that while his soul was departing his body, the devil of vain glory started to praise him saying, "Blessed are you Macarius, you have won", but the saint answered, "I haven't won yet" until his soul reached Paradise. Then, he completed, "Now with the grace of Christ I have arrived to Paradise".

How true are the words of St. John of the Ladder, "Beware of that thief (vain glory) who doesn't leave you up until death."

Pride is a strange sin, which hides itself with virtues so that you cannot easily notice it. The devil of vain glory comes after a person has struggled and conquered so many sins. St John of the Ladder says "If I fast, I am proud of myself, and if I break my fasting to hide my virtue, I am proud of my wisdom. If I wear something new, I like it, and if I wear something old and ragged, I like my ascetism. The same if I speak or be quiet, or if I am praised or disgraced."

Pride dares to appear before everyone, all sins can be hidden in front of others, except pride. It reveals itself so clearly, even in churches. Adulterers, killers and thieves fear disclosure before others, but proud people do not care because they do not feel their mistake and weakness. They always love first seats and love to be in front of everyone in every matter.

All sins share their characteristics with others, except pride. The drunk, adulterer and thief feel happy with their colleagues, but a proud person doesn't want anyone to share his vain glory. He wants to be the only one honoured and loved. Two proud people can never live together. Thus pride deprives me of my good relationship with people, contrary to self denial which strengthens this connectivity. Jesus Son of Sirach says, "Pride is hated by God and people."(Sirach 10: 7)

The Beginning of Sins

Jesus Son of Sirach says, "The beginning of the pride of man, is to fall off from God" (Sirach 10: 12), thus, getting far from God is the beginning of pride. Our relationship with God is like that of a child and his father for we can never do without his care and love. Distancing away from God means we do not need Him because if we feel that God "gives to all life, breath and all things" (Acts 17: 25) how can we live far from Him? Isn't this considered pride?

On the other hand, clinging to God is a proof of our love to Him, and getting far from Him means we do not love Him. How can a person hate and dislike God? Doesn't he fear Him? But again, getting far means that we do not love or fear Him. This is pride.

The Beginning of Sin is Pride, it is the first sin which entered into the world through Satan's envy, and made Adam and Eve fall. Pride is the head and the worst of all sins.

Virtue comes through two routes, either through the fear of God or the love of God. Both routes preserve me from sin. All those who fear God make sure they never disobey Him, and all those who love God keep His Commandments. If I am not following His Commandments out of fear or love, then I am a proud person challenging God and forgetting God's words to Saul, "It is hard for you to kick against the goads" (Acts 9: 5). The same meaning is declared through the Holy Spirit, to the angel of the church of the Laodiceans, "So then, because you are lukewarm, and neither cold nor hot, I will vomit you out of My mouth. Because you say, 'I am rich, have become wealthy, and have need of nothing —and do not know that you are wretched, miserable, poor, blind, and naked". (Rev.3 16, 17) The words "I am rich, have become wealthy and have need of nothing" are a proof of self haughtiness.

Thus, pride has a different meaning according to

God. It is not just haughtiness, being puffed up or seeking people's praise. It includes so many issues which the Wise summarize in the phrase, "Distancing from God."

Beware my brethren of getting spiritually lukewarm, or distancing from your Creator, thinking you do not need Him, "you are wretched, miserable, poor, blind, and naked".

WHAT DOES PRIDE DO?

A proud person is like a daring, arrogant thief who steals from God Himself. He steals the glory, honour, and greatness of the Most Holy. God is zealous about His Glory as mentioned by Isaiah the Prophet, "I am the LORD, that is My name; and My glory I will not give to another." (Is. 42: 8) Similarly, "...I will not give my Glory to another." (Is. 46: 11) St Paul the Apostle says, "Now to the King eternal, immortal, invisible, to God who alone is wise, be honor and glory forever and ever" (Tim.1: 17)

St. Augustine says: "My God, he who seeks praise for something good which he has done is ignoring Your praise and is seeking his own praise because everything is out of your goodness; this one is a thief and a robber, resembling the devil who tried to steal Your Glory."

No wonder the Lord hates this sin more than any other sin. Although God hates evil because it is contrary to His Good Nature, He has a special attitude towards the sin of pride because it is like a tower where all the other sins get shield. St James highlighted this fact, "God resists the proud, but gives grace to the humble." (James 4: 6) This verse clarifies how much God dislikes the proud. He doesn't only reveal His anger towards them but also announces that He resists them.

BAD CONSEQUENCES OF PRIDE:

The Heavenly Grace abandons a proud person because

of his pride and so, he falls in the most horrible sins. The early fathers say: "He who is proud of his knowledge falls in blasphemy, and he who is proud of asceticism falls in adultery." Church history recalls names of heretics such as: Arius, a philosopher and a knowledgable priest; Macdonius and Nastur, who were both Patriarchs of Constantinople and also Eutychus, who was a monastery abbot in a city near Constantinople. Church history likewise mentions great saints and hermits who fell in adultery because of their pride.

A proud person despises God's words as well; "Now it happened, when Jeremiah had stopped speaking to all the people all the words of the LORD their God, for which the LORD their God had sent him to them, all these words, that Azariah the son of Hoshaiah, Johanan the son of Kareah, and all the proud men spoke, saying to Jeremiah, "You speak falsely! The LORD our God has not sent you to say, 'Do not go to Egypt to dwell there." (Jer. 43: 1,2)

Pride removes mercy, kindness and tenderness from one's heart. It blocks the ears from the cry of the needy, closes the eyes from seeing their misery, hardens the hearts and prohibits mercy, "the wicked in his pride persecutes the poor." (Ps. 10: 2)

Pride infuriates disputes amongst people, "by pride comes nothing but strife" (Prov. 13: 10) and "He who is of a proud heart stirs up strife." (Prov.28: 25)

Although some think that they will be great through pride, what happens is always the contrary. God resists the proud and this person never prospers as the Lord says, "whoever exalts himself will be humbled" (Luke 14:

11). The reason is that a proud person is being exalted by himself, not by God, thus he falls and perishes. "He has put down the mighty from their thrones, and exalted the lowly." (Luke 1: 52) Solomon the Wise says, "A man's pride will bring him low, but the humble in spirit will retain honor." (Prov. 29: 23)

God never dwells in a haughy heart, but abandons it. As a result, the heart is ruined and destructed. After the inhabitants of Jerusalem rejected Jesus, the Lord told them: "See, your house is left to you desolate." (Matt. 23: 38) David the Prophet also says, "For I was envious of the boastful, when I saw the prosperity of the wicked... Oh, how they are brought to desolation, as in a moment. They are utterly consumed with terrors as a dream when one awakes, So, Lord, when You awake, You shall despise their image." (Ps. 73:3,19, 20) Solomon the Wise also says, "Pride goes before destruction, and a haughty spirit before a fall."(Prov. 16:18) and "Before destruction, the heart of a man is haughty, and before honor is humility." (Prov.18: 12)

If a person mastered all virtues but offered them to God proudly, God refuses them. It is like incense mixed with dust and dirt. Once it is placed in the censor, a bad smell will come out offending the eyes and nose.

PRIDE AND THE FALL OF THE MIGHTY:

God puts a horrible end to the life of the haughty in order to provide a lesson to others. David the Prophet says, "For You will save the humble people, but will bring down haughty looks. " (Ps. 18: 27) Joshua Son of Sirach says, "The beginning of the pride of man is to fall off from God: Because his heart is departed from Him that made him: for pride is the beginning of all sin, he that holds it shall be filled with maledictions and it shall ruin him in the end." (Sirach 10: 14,15) The Lord says through Isaiah the Prophet, "Behold, the day of the LORD comes, cruel, with both wrath and fierce anger, to lay the land desolate, and He will destroy its sinners from it.... I will punish the world for its evil, and the wicked for their iniquity; I will halt the arrogance of the proud, and will lay low the haughtiness of the terrible." (Is. 13: 9–11)

God humiliated the proud Pharaoh who had fierce animals and wild beasts. He used frogs, lice and flies to show Pharaoh the value of his proud self (Exodus 8). God did the same with Peter His disciple; he humiliated his pride in front of a maid. God humiliated Goliath the arrogant -who reproached the army of the Living God- by David the shepherd who was a young idle lad. David was armoured with God's power, thus repeated "I was brought low and He saved me." (Ps.116: 6)

BIBLE EXAMPLES OF PRIDE

King Nebuchadnezzar of Babylon, "...at the end of the twelve months he was walking about the royal palace of Babylon. The king spoke, saying, "Is not this great Babylon, that I have built for a royal dwelling by my mighty power and for the honor of my majesty?"

While the word was still in the king's mouth, a voice fell from heaven: "King Nebuchadnezzar, to you it is spoken: the kingdom has departed from you! And they shall drive you from men, and your dwelling shall be with the beasts of the field. They shall make you eat grass like oxen; and seven times shall pass over you, until you know that the Most High rules in the kingdom of men, and gives it to whomever He chooses." That very hour the word was fulfilled concerning Nebuchadnezzar; he was driven from men and ate grass like oxen; his body was wet with the dew of heaven till his hair had grown like eagles' feathers and his nails like birds' claws"

After the period assigned by God for his chastisement, he said, "Now I, Nebuchadnezzar, praise and extol and honor the King of heaven, all of whose works are truth, and His ways justice. And those who walk in pride, He is able to put down." (Daniel 4: 19: 36)

The mighty king Herod was stricken by the angel of the Lord; "So on a set day Herod, arrayed in royal apparel, sat on his throne and gave an oration to them. And the people kept shouting, "The voice of a god and not of a man!" Then immediately an angel of the Lord struck him, because he did not give glory to God. And he was eaten by worms and died." (Acts 12: 20-23)

We owe our whole life to God —physically and spiritually- because He is the One Who cares for our bodies and looks after our spirits. As for us, there is nothing good dwelling within us. (Rom.7: 18) How many times do we affront God with our pride and arrogance while "we are dishonoured"!! (1 Cor. 4: 10)

You did not know God by yourself , but He revealed Himself to you. You didn't call Him, but He called you, renewed your life, sanctified your thoughts and chose you to be His own. "He chose us in Him before the foundation of the world, that we should be holy and without blame before Him in love" (Eph. 1: 4)

He prepared a place for you before the foundation of the world. (Matt 25: 34) Don't you know that without the grace of God, you would have drowned in sin and iniquity?

If your thoughts are holy, it is because of God's grace, not for any goodness in you. Generally speaking, if you are feeling spiritually strong, read St. Paul's words, "For it is the God who commanded light to shine out of darkness, who has shone in our hearts to give the light of the knowledge of the glory of God in the face of Jesus Christ. But we have this treasure in earthen vessels that the excellence of the power may be of God and not of us." (2 Cor. 4: 6, 7)

Any good thing in you is from God and any bad thing is from yourself. The bright moon which everyone admires is actually a dark object, receiving its light from the sun. So, can the moon have pride over the sun? What if the sun stopped its light?

Jesus Christ is the Sun of Righteousness and the Light of the World. (Matt. 5: 14) We are getting light from Him so that we can shine. So what would happen to us if He deprives us of His Light? Immediately we will become darkness. We are branches in the True Vine, and the branches are nourished by the roots of the vine. What would happen if the Vine stops providing the branches with nourishment? The branches will dry up, wither quickly, and fall off the Vine.

Rivers do not flow by themselves, but other sources of water are providing for them. Similarly, the river of living water which flows from believers comes out from the work of the Holy Spirit within them. (John 7: 38) What if God stops providing these rivers of living water? It will become dry and would cease to flow. My dear brethren, haven't you read St. James' words: "Every good gift and every perfect gift is from above, and comes down from the Father of lights, with whom there is no variation or shadow of turning." (James 1: 17) St Paul says, "If anyone among you seems to be wise in this age, let him become a fool that he may become wise." (1 Cor 3:18)

You should thank God with all your heart for all the spiritual gifts he has granted you, so that He might keep and increase them. "There is no gift without increase except that without thanksgiving." Thank Him from the depth of your heart even when you feel your weakness, because any good thing in you is from Him. Repeat the beautiful words uttered by St. Gregory the Theologian as he talks to the Incarnate Son in his liturgy "You put in me the talent of speaking. You gave me the knowledge to know You, to bound me to all the paths leading to life. You blessed my nature in Yourself. You completed the Law on my behalf. You showed me how to stand after my fall."

St. Paul had so many spiritual gifts. He saw many heavenly revelations; "It is doubtless not profitable for me to boast. I will come to visions and revelations of the Lord." (2 Cor. 12: 1) When he wanted to inform the believers of what he had seen in the third heaven, he didn't talk about himself but with great self denial he said, "I know a man in Christ who fourteen years ago—whether in the body I do not know, or whether out of the body I do not know, God knows—such a one was caught up to the third heaven. And I know such a man—whether in the body or out of the body I do not know, God knows— how he was caught up into Paradise and heard inexpressible words, which it is not lawful for a man to utter." (2 Cor. 12: 2-4) He continues to say, "Of such a one I will boast; yet of myself I will not boast, except in my infirmities." (2 Cor. 12: 5) Again, "And He said to me, "My grace is sufficient for you, for My strength is made perfect in weakness." Therefore most gladly I will rather boast in my infirmities, that the power of Christ may rest upon me. Therefore I take pleasure in infirmities, in reproaches, in needs, in persecutions, in distresses, for Christ's sake. For when I am weak, then I am strong." (2 Cor. 12: 9-10)

REASONS LEADING TO PRIDE

There are many reasons which lead to pride. The devil uses them as weapons to fight against us.

PERSONAL REASONS:

Such as beauty, intelligence, good health, physical strength…..etc. It is really strange that these beautiful gifts would be a reason for our pride. They were granted to us totally by God, but instead of giving God the glory, we tease Him!! St Paul says, "He who glories, let him glory in the Lord." (1 Cor. 1: 31) Also "If I must boast, I will boast in the things which concern my infirmity." (2 Cor.

11-30) Do you have a hand in how pretty you look, how strong you are or how intelligent? These gifts were granted to you, in addition to many others like social success and richness. We have to thank God as He is the One Who granted them to us. If you have a pleasant personality, don't think it is because of your ability in dealing with others. Be sure that it is God who gave you grace in the eyes of others.

You can never guarantee the permanency of these gifts. Your beauty might be deformed one day because of illness or accident. You can lose your memory. The same applies to general health. How many strong people fell into severe illness and became weak and helpless?

Let's say that these gifts lasted with you till the end of your life. Would they be of any benefit for you infront of the Just Judge on Judgement Day? He will judge according to the state of the heart not the outer appearance.

WORLDLY REASONS:

Richness, positions, might, authority... etc.

This is a fruitful field for the devil of pride. St Paul says, "But those who desire to be rich fall into temptation and a snare, and into many foolish and harmful lusts which drown men in destruction and perdition. For the love of money is a root of all kinds of evil, for which some have strayed from the faith in their greediness, and pierced themselves through with many sorrows. But you, O man of God, flee these things and pursue righteousness, godliness, faith, love, patience, gentleness..." (1 Tim. 6: 9-11) Also, "By your great wisdom in trade you have increased your riches, and your heart is lifted up because of your riches."(Ez. 28: 5)

Do these, rich, mighty, people know that God is the source of these authorities and that He is the only Giver of power? Hannah, Samuel's mother said, "The Lord makes poor and makes rich; he brings low and lifts up. He raises the poor from the dust and lifts the beggar from the ash heap, to set them among princes and make them inherit the throne of glory." (1 Sam. 2: 7,8) Also, "And you shall remember the Lord your God, for it is He who gives you power to get wealth." (Deut. 8: 18)

How wonderful is the meek praise of St. Mary when she went to St. Elizabeth, "He has shown strength with His arm; He has scattered the proud in the imagination of their hearts. He has put down the mighty from their thrones, and exalted the lowly. He has filled the hungry with good things, and the rich He has sent away empty." (Luke 1: 51-53)

Nothing is better for a person than to be rich with God and rich in good deeds. This is St Paul's recommendation to Timothy his disciple, "Command those who are rich in this present age not to be haughty, nor to trust in uncertain riches but in the living God, who gives us richly all things to enjoy. Let them do good, that they be rich in good works, ready to give, willing to share, storing up for themselves a good foundation for the time to come, that they may lay hold on eternal life." (1 Tim. 6: 17-19)

Worldly matters are vain and never permanent. A good example from the Holy Bible is Job the Righteous, about whom it is written, "So that this man was the greatest of all the people of the east." (Job 1: 3) Job lost everything in a very short time: his wealth, his children and all his slaves. This fulfills Solomon's words, "...for riches are not forever." (Prov. 27: 24) Even if you can hold them during your entire life here on earth, you can never take any of them hereafter.

People may honour you because of your richness and high position, but things will change in eternity. There, you will be like everyone else, naked, as Job the Righteous said; " Naked I came from my mother's womb, and naked shall I return there. The Lord gave, and the Lord has taken away; Blessed be the name of the Lord."(Job 1: 21)

Richness did not benefit the rich man on whose door Lazarus used to beg, stricken with wounds and poverty. Our father Abraham said to him, "Son, remember that in your lifetime you received your good things, and likewise Lazarus evil things; but now he is comforted and you are tormented." (Luke 16: 19-25)

Don't gather money for the sake of getting rich, thinking that it will make people respect and love you. Instead, discover "the hidden treasure" and obtain "the one expensive pearl." Have Christ and then you will own the whole world as said by St. Paul "as sorrowful, yet always rejoicing; as poor, yet making many rich; as having nothing, and yet possessing all things." (2 Cor. 6: 10) Ask yourself honestly where your treasure is; because the Lord Jesus says, "for where your treasure is, there your heart will be also."

Pious Reasons:

Pride hides itself within other virtues. That is why there is no wonder that pious reasons could lead to pride. An example is a person who is crowned with spiritual virtues, or special gifts such as teaching, preaching, nice voice in church tunes, etc. All our pious practices are in vain and God rejects them if they are accompanied by pride and haughtiness. David the prophet says: "The sacrifices of God are a broken spirit, a broken and a contrite heart— These, O God, You will not despise." (Ps. 51: 17)

In Luke 18: 9-14, we read about the Pharisee who depended on his self rightousness, his fastings, prayers, alms giving and other virtues. All of which were rejected by God because he offered them in pride and arrogance.

Social Reasons:

Praise and admiration of others, excessive respect and generosity offered to us by them.

These are very active and successful traps set by the devil to catch those who are struggling in the path of virtues. St John of the Ladder says, "He is really a great person who despises the praise of people, and greater is he who despises the praise of the devils." When we accept praise, immediately we fall into the sin of vain glory which directly leads us into pride.

One might say: "I know I am nothing but I can't stop people from praising and respecting me. Isn't it great to encourage good deeds so that people might enhance in goodness?"

I agree with you that you can't control peoples' emotions towards you, but you can control your own. How do you feel when people praise and admire you? Don't you feel inner happiness and satisfaction? Doesn't it sound good in your ears? Don't you love them more and more, even though you feel like a sinner? Isn't it God who is working within you?

It could go even further. When someone asks for peoples' opinion in regards to a service, they may say humble phrases and expressions to gain praise. This is indeed the devil of vain glory. So beware of this attitude otherwise the weeds of pride will begin shooting inside your heart.

The early fathers were very cautious about this matter by saying, "He who praises his brethren is setting a trap for himself." Also, "Do not praise a person in his presence lest he get puffed up, and do not praise a person while he is away lest you infuriate the devils' envy againt him."

Flee from praise, live as a dead person in this world, because the world is passing away and the lust of it. (1 John 2: 17) Don't care much about the praise or insult of others. Don't rejoice if they praise you or get upset if they vilify you. Nothing changes anything in your life. Accept insult, ridicule and vilifying because it heals against vain glory. This is the path the saints treaded through and it was definately a narrow door. St Isaac says "Don't consider it a day of your life if it passed without any ridicule."

Who are you to accept praise and glory from others, while your Master and Teacher says, "I do not receive honour from men." (John 5: 41) If these are the words of the Holy Who is without sin, what would I say when I am "brought forth in iniquity, and in sin my mother conceived me"?

Don't you know that people praise and admire you because they only see the nice side of your personality? They know nothing about your sins, iniquities, weaknesses or wrong doings because the Merciful Loving Lord is hiding them and covering you! That's why we start our prayers with the Thanksgiving Prayer "Let us give thanks to the beneficent and merciful God, the Father of our Lord, God and Savior, Jesus Christ, for He has covered us, helped us, guarded us, accepted us unto Him, spared us, supported us, and brought us to this hour." We thank Him for "covering us" before we thank Him for helping us, guarding us, accepting us, etc.

If this is the case my dear, how can you forget and accept others' praise and glory?

Devilish Reasons:

These are a result of the devils' fights to make us sin. After one conquers his/her weaknesses, the devil attempts to fight via praise. The devil of pride always disguises in virtues. He attempts to steal all the fruits of many years of struggle.

Our early fathers were so cautious about this trick. In one case, the devil appeared in the shape of a luminous angel to one of the fathers saying, "I am Gabriel sent to you." However, the father immediately said, "Probably you are sent to someone else, because I am a sinner."

The devils used to appear to a certain father and

when Satan was tired of his piety, he appeared to him in a luminous shape saying "I am Christ." The elder closed his eyes, and the devil said "Christ is standing here and you are closing your eyes?" The saint answered, "I don't want to see Christ here on earth!"

In both stories, the devil couldn't stand the humility of the fathers and so disappeared immediately.

COMPARING OURSELVES TO OTHERS:

Pride occurs when one compares himself to another of lower spiritual status.

This is a dangerous weapon used by Satan, in an attempt to stop our struggle and keep us satisfied with what we have reached. Here we ask: Why compare yourself to those who are less and not compare yourself to the saints and those of higher spiritual and intellectual levels?

If you are falling into this trick, you are decreasing your struggle and restricting your active strife. God wants us to be perfect and saintly. It is not a recommendation, but an order , "Therefore you shall be perfect, just as your Father in heaven is perfect." (Matt. 5: 48) Furthermore, "But as He who called you is Holy, you also be holy in all your conduct." (1 Peter 1: 15)

"Pursue peace with all people, and holiness, without which no one will see the Lord" (Heb. 12: 14) The Bible also says: "the righteous one is scarcely saved." (1 Peter 4:18) Therefore those who are lukewarm and reluctant are hated by God as He says, "So then, because you are lukewarm, and neither cold nor hot, I will vomit you out of My mouth." (Rev.3: 16) So why aren't we keen about our struggle? Why are we satisfied with our current stale situation, feeling that –thank God- we are much better than others?

Look at the lives of the great saints, the apostles, the martyrs, the confessors and all those who struggled. Look at the Apostles: St Paul and St. Mark. Look at the martyrs: St. George, St. Mina, St. Barbara and St. Demiana. Look at the ascetic monks: St. Paul, St. Anthony, St. Macarius, St. Arsanius, St. Pachomius and St. Shenouda.

If we put the lives of these saints before our eyes, and consider their love, struggle and asceticism, our hearts will inflame with love and holy zeal, and we will discover how little we are. We will shout out, "If the righteous one is scarcely saved, where shall I the sinner appear?"

Pride in one's own Eyes

According to St Anthony, discernment precedes all virtues and is the light which enlightens the whole body. According to the saints, discernment is attained through humility and discovering one's true self. Now be honest with yourself and answer the following questions:

- From the depth of your heart, do you feel that you are nothing without God and that all good things in you are coming from God?

- How do you feel when you pray before God, whether alone or with others? Do you feel unworthy to stand before Him like the tax-collector, "And the tax collector, standing afar off, would not so much as raise his eyes to heaven, but beat his breast, saying, 'God, be merciful to me a sinner!'" (Luke 18: 13)

- If you are serving at church, do you feel that you are giving or taking? Do you feel you are sacrificing your time and effort to serve God, or do you thank Him for giving you the chance to pass His words and teachings to others? Do you feel unworthy to teach? Do you feel as though you are the one needing to be taught? Do you feel that you are sitting on the Teacher's chair or do you feel like you are sitting at His Feet to learn?

- How do you feel when you are fasting? Do you feel proud and happy when you abstain till a late hour? Are you fasting so that people do not mock you? Are you fasting for your weaknesses or for your spiritual growth? Do you feel that abstaining till a late hour is for chastising your crooked self? Do you feel that your fasting can't be compared to other pious peoples' fasting? Do you fast from committing sins?

- How do you feel with charitable deeds? Do you feel you've done your duty towards God giving the tithes and following His orders? Do you do this to get praised by others, and "sound a trumpet before you as the hypocrites do in the synagogues and in the streets", or do you make sure: "do not let your left hand know what your right hand is doing, that your charitable deed may be in secret; and your Father who sees in secret will Himself reward you openly." (Matt.6: 1-4)

- As for the quantity, do you know that giving

tithes is the minimum standard according to the Old Testament? Yet in the New Testament, Lord Jesus Christ teaches us to take a step further by "(selling) what (we) have and (giving) alms" (Luke 12: 33). St. Paul says, "For we brought nothing into this world, and it is certain we can carry nothing out. And having food and clothing, with these we shall be content." (1 Timothy 6: 7, 8). The Apostle also asked us to be generous in giving, "But this I say: He who sows sparingly will also reap sparingly, and he who sows bountifully will also reap bountifully. So let each one give as he purposes in his heart, not grudgingly or of necessity; for God loves a cheerful giver. And God is able to make all grace abound toward you, that you, always having all sufficiency in all things, may have an abundance for every good work. As it is written:

" He has dispersed abroad,

He has given to the poor;

His righteousness endures forever" (2 Cor.9: 6-9)

- The money which you are giving as alms is not yours, but God's. He is the One Who gave it to you. Then, what is your almsgiving worth compared to those who offered their wealth and lives as well, "They were stoned, they were sawn in two, were tempted, were slain with the sword. They wandered about in sheepskins and goatskins, being destitute, afflicted, tormented— of whom the world was not worthy. They wandered in deserts and mountains, in dens and caves of the earth." (Heb. 11: 37-38)

- Generally speaking, test your heart and inner emotions, uproot pride, so that the roots of virtues may grow and give fruits. Jesus Son of Sirach says, "Extol not yourself in the thoughts of your soul like a bull; lest your strength be quashed by folly, and it eat up your leaves and destroy your fruit; and you will be left as a dry tree in the wilderness." (Sirach 6: 2,3)

CHARACTERISTICS OF PRIDE

We've mentioned previously that a person might feel proud, although appearing humble in front of others. However, pride can always be reflected in one's outer appearance. For example, the way he walks, what he wears, the volume of his voice and his dealings with others.

However, I need to attract your attention to three main points:

Firstly: We should not judge people depending on outer appearance, as the Lord warned us against this, saying, "Do not judge according to appearance, but judge with righteous judgment." (John 7: 24)

Secondly: The devil might make use of the situation by dragging us into Judgment. Judgment is the daughter of pride.

Thirdly: It is not always the case that one with these features is proud. We have to examine ourselves deeply so that we might not become a stumbling block to others, losing their love and friendship.

A proud person may walk in a haughty style. We have to remember that we are stepping on deceased people whose bodies became dust hundreds of years ago. Our bodies my dear brethren, which we are proud of, will also, become dust one day. "Why is earth and ashes proud?" (Sirach 10: 10)

Pride might appear through expensive clothing, ornaments and excessive stylish wear. Remember the Apostles' words, "...and having food and clothing, with these we shall be content." (1 Tim. 6: 8). As a meek son, follow Your Meek Lord, who didn't have any money to pay for taxes. (Matt. 17: 24-27) Although He is The Owner of heaven and earth, He became poor voluntarily, and had "nowhere to lay his head." (Matt.8: 20)

Pride might appear in the way a person talks, whether he talks with authority, talks loudly or always gives orders. Examine yourself my dear brethren. Resemble Your Master about Whom it is said, "...He will not quarrel nor cry out, Nor will anyone hear His voice in the streets. A bruised reed He will not break, and smoking flax He will not quench." (Matt. 12:19-20) Don't talk with authority, but talk in meekness, even in situations where you have to give orders. Choose your words when you are angry as it is written, "be angry and do not sin." (Eph.4: 26)

Pride Disguised in Virtue

A Good Role Model:

When one tries hard to achieve virtues, the devil attacks him, convincing him that he has to be a role model and a light to the world. He even quotes words from the

Holy Bible to assure his deceit, "Let your light so shine before men, that they may see your good works and glorify your Father in heaven." (Matt.5: 16). As a result, the person changes his attitude before people in order to be a role model and "fulfill the commandments" by spreading the kingdom of God on earth. This is a deceitful fight coming from the devil. Instead of aiming at God, our worship is aimed at people. People praise and honour us, thus, we receive our reward on earth and lose our reward in heaven.

This is not the same as hypocrisy as a hypocrite is a person who pretends to be pious, but is full of iniquities from inside. According to the Apostle, "having the image of piety but denying its power."

But the case we are discussing here is a person who really wants to be pious and is struggling to acquire virtues, yet he gets deceived with Satan's tricks and pleases people instead. "Bondservants, obey in all things your masters according to the flesh, not with eye service, as men-pleasers, but in sincerity of heart, fearing God. And whatever you do, do it heartily, as to the Lord and not to men, knowing that from the Lord you will receive the reward of the inheritance; for you serve the Lord Christ." (Col.3: 22 – 24)

If the devil of vain glory fights you with verses from the Holy Bible –as he dared and did with your Master- throw arrows of humility at him, and fight him with "the sword of the Spirit which is the Word of God." (Eph. 6: 17) David the Psalmist says, "Happy is the man who has his quiver full of them." (Ps.127: 5)

St. John of the Ladder says: "Do not listen to the devil of vain glory especially when he suggests you disclose your virtues so that others might benefit." Remember the Lord's words, "For what profit is it to a man if he gains the whole world, and loses his own soul?" (Matt. 16: 26)

Don't be a Stumble to Others:

The devil of Pride might disguise himself under the motto 'Don't be a stumble to others.' As a result, you try not to sin in front of others, thus you act pious to show off to others, rather than to God. We have to avoid evil out of love for God, not to act righteous in the eyes of others.

Sometimes we defend ourselves when we are accused of a wrong doing. This is inner pride because we do not want to appear weak or mistaken before others.

Always remember that your Master, "Was oppressed and He was afflicted, yet He opened not His mouth." (Is. 53: 7) Always remember the saints who remained patient even though they were falsely accused of many things. They never defended themselves and thus defeated their mightiest enemies. For example, St. Macarius the Great was accused of having a relationship with a girl who later got pregnant. This saint tolerated so many insults, ridicules and hits and never said a word to defend himself. Instead, he worked harder, telling himself, "You have to toil Maqqara, now you have a wife." However, the girl experienced much difficulty during child labour that she confessed the identity of the other person whom she committed adultery with. When her family went to apologize and honour St. Macarius, he had already fled to the inner wilderness to avoid vain glory and praise.

We are not mentioning this story to encourage you to deny your rights when you are wrongly accused. In fact, there is no Divine commandment denying this right. However, we need to attract our attention to the wonderful attitude of the saints, who humbled themselves extensively to avoid vain glory. Therefore, you should not get angry and care much about defending yourself in trifle matters because in this way, you are responding to the devil of Pride, who always disguises himself in the robe of Self defense.

DEFENDING THE TRUTH AND CORRECT PRINCIPLES:

A person might get aggressive in defending the truth, yet people have to know that the truth fights for itself, without loudness or stubbornness. A person might defend the truth out of personal pride, arrogance and superiority.

A person might be strict in a certain spiritual principle. Yet, the danger lies when he thinks that his opinion is the sole correct one and everyone else is wrong. This is called 'The pride of principles'. There are many ways to serve God and reach Him; all of these means complete each other.

THE HIGH SOCIAL OR SPIRITUAL POSITION:

Sometimes those who are in high social or spiritual positions think that they have to appear proud and haughty to befit their positions, but actually, the devil of

Pride is the initiative of this idea. If being humble exalts us to heaven, won't it exalt us in the eyes of people living on earth?

If St. James the Apostle says, "God resists the proud, but gives grace to the humble" (James 4:6), so wouldn't God give us grace in the eyes of people out of love and respect? God was never a proud person. When He was Incarnate, He put on the robe of humility and hid His Divinity, yet everyone respected Him. His humility never decreased His honour or dignity.

If humility is an essential trait for a person in any high position, it is even more essential to those in church positions. St Origen says, "Many priests forget all about humility after their ordination, as if they have been ordained priests in order to stop being humble!! In fact, it is the other way round, they should increase in humility as said, "The greater you are, the more humble you should be, and you shall find grace before God." (Sirach 3: 20) If the church has chosen you, bow your head in humility. If you are in a leading position, don't be proud, but act as a member of the whole body. You have to be humble. You have to be ridiculed. You have to escape pride because it is the head of all vices."

Pride doesn't add any honour or respect, but what does so is the spirituality of that person, especially in church positions. On the other hand, pride makes him fall because it doesn't befit a church leader or minister.

GENERALLY SPEAKING ABOUT PRIDE:

Some people are not just proud of personal gifts. They

become proud of their family or the religious society they belong to like the church they attend and the Sunday school class they teach. In fact, being proud of such matters reveals inner pride, superficial thinking and a lack of spiritual depth. St Paul rebuked the Corinthians saying, "For when one says, "I am of Paul," and another, "I am of Apollos," are you not carnal? Therefore let no one boast in men." (1 Cor. 3: 4, 21) He also told the Galatians, "For if anyone thinks himself to be something, when he is nothing, he deceives himself. But let each one examine his own work, and then he will have rejoicing in himself alone, and not in another. For each one shall bear his own load." (Gal. 6: 3-5).

Do not boast in anything, except in the Lord, as it is written, "He who glories, let him glory in the LORD."(1 Cor. 1: 31).

Do not be proud for serving in a particular church or for having a renounced position in Sunday School service. This will not save you or be of any benefit before the Just Judge in Judgment Day. Be proud in Jesus Christ alone and repeat with David the Psalmist, "My soul shall make its boast in the Lord." (Ps. 34: 2).

Our real pride is that we are the children of God. We feel even prouder to see His Blessed Name glorified in the mouths of many people. We feel proud that the Lord is reigning over our hearts and minds.

How Can a Person Cure His Pride?

Relate Good Deeds to the Work of Grace:

Always feel that any good thing in you is coming from God; "Then God saw everything that He had made, and indeed, it was very good." (Gen.1: 31) Repeat with Daniel the Prophet, "O Lord, righteousness belongs to you, but to us shame of face." (Dan. 9: 7) Don't get deceived with the glittering glory of the world or its temporary sweetness for it is followed with poison and bitterness. Renounce the world, for the world will pass away and all its desires.

Hide your Virtues:

If the Lord has granted you virtues, don't talk about them before others, even if you have gained them after hard struggle. Always remember, "So likewise you, when you have done all those things which you are commanded, say, 'We are unprofitable servants. We have done what was our duty to do.'" (Luke 17: 10) Hide your virtues so that they may grow. They are like a treasure. If you reveal it, it gets stolen. Moses' mother hid her son for three months, and so is the case with the virtue. If we do not hide it from our spiritual Pharaoh –Satan- it will never grow. The saints of our Church always hid their virtues. Some even acted insane. When they had to retell spiritual experiences, they spoke as though speaking of others.

If you reveal your virtues in an attempt for praise, you have already received your reward in this lifetime. (Luke 16: 25) When Lord Jesus Christ talked about the hypocrites, who loved to pray standing in synagogues and on the corners of the streets that they may be seen by men, He says, "Assuredly, I say to you, they have their reward." (Matt. 6: 5)

Dignity

x

"He who seeks dignity will not find it, but he who escapes it knowingly, dignity will follow him and guide people to where he is."

(St. Isaac the Syrain)

- Christianity and the Dignity of Human Beings
- Why should I flee the glory of the world?
- How can I have true dignity?

Christianity and the Dignity of Human Beings

Dignity has many meanings in our daily life. It can be expressed positively through servants, parents, teachers or elders as they give glory to God. It can be expressed negitavely when one seeks self glory. Alleged dignity occurs through cruel actions like hitting or killing as a result of revenge or humiliation. For many years, dignity has disrupted people in their work and sleep by stealing away their inner peace. It has deprived them from the spirit of forgiveness and replaced them with emotions of worry, envy and complaint. It even leads to legal actions.

Now, we will concentrate on personal dignity which is sought after by many people. It is the wrong kind of dignity because of its motives.

Worldly Dignity is a Daughter of Pride

Worldly dignity is a result of pride and haughtiness, because it aims to obtain personal dignity and even fight for it. A true Christian person is one who takes off the robe of worldly dignity, and puts on the robe of humility, immitating his Master. Thus, he doesn't care about worldly dignity, "We are fools for Christ's sake, but you are wise in Christ! We are weak, but you are strong! You are distinguished, but we are dishonored!" (1 Cor. 4: 10)

Worldly dignity causes a person to get furious, "for the wrath of man does not produce the righteousness of God." (James 1: 20) He then loses his meekness, becoming estranged from his Meek Master Who asks us to resemble Him in order to find rest (Matt.11: 29). Disguised under dignity, a person claims he cannot give up his rights as this will lessen his dignity; he gets more and more infuriated and things quickly worsen.

CHRISTIANITY AND DIGNITY

Does this mean that Christianity decreases one's dignity and allows him to be humiliated by others? Does it mean one cannot make a move to defend his situation?

Christianity honours mankind and considers him the crown of creation, however, it is a religion which aims to create a spiritual community by eradicating the spirit of evil from man, and taking them back to their original form before sin, when God created man in His image and likeness. (Gen. 1: 26) Christianity teaches us to love our enemies, to bless those who curse us, to do good to those who hate us and to pray for those who hurt us (Matt. 4: 44), so that these people may become our friends. Dignity gives us a strong weapon by which we conquer our enemies; it is the weapon of goodness which eradicates the roots of evil, "Do not be overcome by evil, but overcome evil with good." (Romans 12: 21). Thus, tolerance is a result of power not of weakness, because "He who is slow to anger is better than the mighty and he who rules his spirit than he who takes a city". (Prov.16: 32)

This is very clear in our personal life. Although some people think it is humiliating to follow these commandments, it actually adds to a man's dignity and appreciation, through means of love and meekness. Consequently, turning enemies to beloved ones, and rivals to friends.

This also applies in public and political life. Ghandi, the Indian leader, proved that these positive principals lead to positive results. Removing the mountains of hatred and paving hearts with love and humbleness are the work of a strong person, not one without dignity. No one ever said that Ghandi was a weak or insane person; on the contrary, they considered him a hero who challenged the mighty British Empire without weapons.

If a girl is killed after committing adultery, and the killer claims that it was to regain the family's dignity, it is still classed a murder. He cannot cast out a sick member who can be treated. Our Master Lord Jesus Christ acted differently in similar situations for He gave sinners a chance for repentance, transforming them into saintly servants.

God Avenges for His Children's Dignity:

What we mentioned above relates to personal dignity within the teachings of Christianity. We do not punish others for misinterpreting "dignity", but we enrich their souls to gain true "dignity." There is another divine aspect to this issue, which makes us stop avenging ourselves, as God takes care of His children. He avenges us, humiliates our enemies and persecutors, and repays us dignity twofold.

This is no wonder, because He says, "He who rejects you, rejects Me." (Luke 10: 16) Therefore, if God directs our rejection and insult to Himself, wouldn't He avenge for us and redeem our dignity?!

St. Paul the Apostle says, "It is a righteous thing with God to repay with tribulation those who trouble you." (2 Thes. 1: 6)

During David's time, the Cushite came and said to him, "There is good news, my lord the king! For the LORD has avenged you this day of all those who rose against you." (2 Sam. 18: 31)

Before crossing the Red Sea, Moses told the Israelites, "Do not be afraid. Stand still, and see the salvation of the LORD, which He will accomplish for you today... The Lord will fight for you, and you shall hold your peace." (Ex. 14: 13, 14) Do not seek dignity; let the heavens proclaim your dignity.

A Story

During World War I, a saintly priest in Upper Egypt asked a favour from the mayor of the village. However, the mayor was an aggressive person who mistreated the priest and slapped him on the face. The priest left quite upset and headed to his church (St. George church) where he started his prayer service. During this time, while the mayor was walking in the street, a knight mounting a horse met him and asked him about the reason for humiliating the priest. Before the mayor had a chance to answer, the knight slapped him on the face. The hit was so powerful that he lost vision in one of his eyes. The knight was St. George who disappeared immediately.

Another Story:

During the vigil praises of Kiahk, a priest who served

in St. Philopateer Merkorious (Abu Sefein) Church in Upper Egypt, was heading to the church, while a robber named Bilal stopped him and asked him for money. When the priest informed him that he had no money, the robber grabbed the priest by force and slapped him fiercely on his face.

The priest later arrived at the church and continued with the rest of the congregation in prayer and praise. Suddenly, they heard the sound of a gunshot, and people started screaming "Bilal is shot dead." Surprisingly, after police investigation, they could not find the bullet which killed Bilal or any evidence of crime. It was very clear that it was a miraculous shot avenging the priest's dignity.

The Lord proclaims our dignity and doubles it when we are silent. The Lord has His miraculous ways, which we cannot perform. Do not think you are merely a person ignored by God. In fact, you are His beloved one and He honors you more than any other creation.

MAN IS GREATER THAN ANY OTHER CREATION:

You are the only eternal creature created in the image and likeness of God. You have dominion over every living thing that moves on earth, "Then God blessed them, and God said to them, "Be fruitful and multiply; fill the earth and subdue it; have dominion over the fish of the sea, over the birds of the air, and over every living thing that moves on the earth." (Gen. 1: 28)

You lost power over beasts and fierce animals after you sinned and you lost control on your own self. You can still regain this control if you free yourself from sin, just like the saints who tamed and lived with wild beasts and animals. You are the only one beautified by mind and speech and the only one in whom God is delighted, "and my delight was with the son of man." (Pr. 8: 31) You are the one whom God washed. You are the one whom God gave His Body and Blood so that you may abide in Him, a gift that the angels yearn for.

You are the one on whom God is knocking at your door, waiting for you to open so that He may come and dine with you. (Rev 3: 20, John 14: 23) You have authority to trample on serpents and scorpions, and over all the power of the enemy. You are the one about whom the Lord says, "Assuredly, I say to you, whatever you bind on earth will be bound in heaven, and whatever you loose on earth will be loosed in heaven." (Matt. 18: 18)

You are the one about whom the Lord says, "In My Father's house are many mansions; if it were not so, I would have told you. I go to prepare a place for you. And if I go and prepare a place for you, I will come again and receive you to Myself; that where I am, there you may be also." (John 14: 2, 3)

You are the one sitting at the King's banquet, "If anyone serves Me, let him follow Me; and where I am, there My servant will be also. If anyone serves Me, him My Father will honor." (John 12: 26)

The Apostle says, "Do you not know that your bodies are members of Christ?" (1 Cor. 6: 15) You are the only one about whom it is said, "Do you not know that you are the temple of God and that the Spirit of God dwells in you?" (1 Cor.3: 16)

You are the only one about whom the Lord says, "Most assuredly, I say to you, he who believes in Me, the works that I do he will do also; and greater works than these he will do." (John 14: 12)

GOD WAS INCARNATED AND SUFFERED FOR THE SAKE OF MAN:

O my Lord, the wide heavens cannot contain You, yet You dwelled in the womb of The Virgin for my sake, being born in a manger, like one without home or residence. You are the Creator of heaven and earth, the Resort of the entire world. Although You are the source of richness and luxury, You were wrapped in old rags and laid on the dust in the manger, like the poorest person.

They carried You and fled, even though You are the Harbour of the weary and fugitive. Although You are the Giver of Life, You were persecuted like someone sentenced to death. You were baptised in water in order to sanctify me, while You are the Holy of holies. You tolerated mockery and humiliation in order to honor me. You drank bitter and vinegar to give me sweetness, even though I willingly drank bitterness from the devil's hand.

You yielded to death willingly to protect me, "For He made Him Who knew no sin to be sin for us, that we might become the righteousness of God in Him." (2 Cor. 5: 21)

MAN IS THE SON OF GOD, WHOM THE ANGELS ARE SERVING:

My brethren, you are conformed to the image of the Son of God, "For whom He foreknew, He also predestined to be conformed to the image of His Son, that He might be the firstborn among many brethren." (Rom.8: 29) You are the beloved of God. He gave you the honour to be called His brethren, and said to Mary Magdalene after His Resurrection, "Go to My brethren and say to them..." (John 20: 17) You have an assigned angel to protect you; you are the one whom the angel of the Lord encamps around and protects. (Ps 34: 7) You are the one served by the angels, "Sent forth to minister for those who will inherit salvation" (Heb.1: 14). The angels rejoiced for your salvation and announced it to the shepherds. (Luke 2: 8-14)

You are the one whom the angels serve. They support you in your troubles, shut the mouths of lions, quench the flames of fire, ask and intercede on your behalf.

You are very precious and honourable. Christianity honours and uplifts your humanity through divine dignity, rather than worldly dignity.

Why Should I Flee the Glory of the World?

There are two kinds of dignity: divine dignity and worldly dignity. So, what is worldly dignity and why should we flee it?

IT IS TRIVIAL AND VOID:

No matter how glittering and attracting the world's dignities are, they are just mirages. We see it from afar and consider it our target, but we will never reach it because it is just a mirage.

They are trivial matters compared to the true dignity given by God. For this reason, Jesus Son of Sirach says, "Seek not of the Lord a pre-eminence, nor of the king the seat of honour." (Sirach 7: 4)

Any form of dignity offered by the world, whether words of praise, high positions or richness, are all vain matters.

King Solomon received all riches and honor, "And I have also given you what you have not asked: both riches and honor, so that there shall not be anyone like you among the kings all your days."(1 Kings 3: 13)

King Solomon gave us his experiences regarding riches and honor by saying: "Vanity of vanities, all is vanity... I, the Preacher, was king over Israel in Jerusalem. And I set my heart to seek and search out by wisdom concerning all that is done under heaven; this burdensome task God has given to the sons of man, by which they may be exercised. I have seen all the works that are done under the sun; and indeed, all is vanity and grasping for the wind." (Ecc.1: 2, 12-14).

He also says, "I communed with my heart, saying, 'Look, I have attained greatness, and have gained more wisdom than all who were before me in Jerusalem. My heart has understood great wisdom and knowledge.' And I set my heart to know wisdom and to know madness and folly. I perceived that this also is grasping for the wind. For in much wisdom is much grief, And he who increases knowledge increases sorrow."(Ecc. 1: 16-18), and "Whatever my eyes desired I did not keep from them. I did not withhold my heart from any pleasure, For my heart rejoiced in all my labor; And this was my reward from all my labor. Then I looked on all the works that my hands had done, And on the labor in which I had toiled; And indeed all was vanity and grasping for the wind. There was no profit under the sun." (Ecc.2: 10-11)

Now, my brethren, think about King Solomon's words. Can you imagine excelling him by any means?

It is temporary:

The honours of the world are short lived. Satan showed the Lord Jesus "all the kingdoms of the world in a moment of time." (Luke 4: 5) Yes, in just a moment of time; which makes us feel how fast the glories of the world can go!

People celebrated the Lord Jesus as KING on Palm Sunday, crying out "Hosanna." However, four days later, they shouted: "Crucify Him" in front of Pontius Pilate.

In addition to being short, the glories of the world are temporary. Those who are honored usually put on their best clothes and ornaments for the celebration, but when it is bedtime, they take them off for they cannot get rest while wearing these costumes. Same with us, the night of our life will soon come and then, unwillingly, we will have to take off all vain things. It is much better to take them off willingly while we are still alive rather than unwillingly at the time of departure.

St. Anthony looked at his dead father and said, "You left the world unwillingly, but I will leave it willingly."

We can never take worldly honor with us into eternal life because the gate of the Kingdom is narrow and can only fit the naked, "naked I came from my mother's womb, and naked shall I return there." (Job 1: 21] If we will all stand before Christ, naked, tell me my friend, how can you differentiate between the educated and the illiterate, the poor and the rich?

It is surrounded by danger:

St. John Chrysostom says, "A leader worries a lot." Also "I wonder for the leader who could be saved." This is because of the many dangers surrounding the glories, praises and preeminent positions of the world. The more a person is elevated in position and in society, the more responsibilities he is tied to and the harder it is to maintain one's salvation. In addition, there are numerous problems that choke this person. On top of all this, comes the war of pride from the devil of vain glory.

"Worldly honour" endangers our life in eternity. St.Jerome says, "It is very hard for a person to enjoy good things both in this world and in the world to come. It is hard to experience both earthly joys and everlasting eternal joys. It is hard to be honoured here and there."

When Joseph presented his two sons, Ephraim and Manasseh, to Jacob, he made the eldest Ephraim stand on Jacob's right hand and Manasseh the younger on his left. This was according to the protocol that the eldest child receives most honour. Yet, Jacob crossed his hands and put his right hand on Manasseh's head and his left hand on Ephraim's head.

That is what God will do on Judgement Day. He will lead those who were most humble and humiliated in this world. The Lord explained this in detail through the Parable of the rich man and Lazarus (Luke 16: 19-31). The honour was reversed after they died. Lazarus who desired to be fed with the crumbs falling from the rich man's table, was now being asked to dip the tip of his finger in water and cool the tongue of the rich man.

It deprives us from God's blessings:

St. Paul the Apostle says, "for Demas has forsaken me, having loved this present world." (2 Tim.4: 10)

The glories of this world often attracted the children of God, pulling them away from the Truth. They are like waterfalls. If you approach them, they will drag you in and drown you. They are like a magnet. If you come across its field, it will pull you within and destroy the characteristics that make you the child of God. They are like a piece of iron placed in a magnet wave. The iron gets attracted to the magnet and gains the magnetic characteristic! Thus, the glories of the world will always deprive us of the blessings of God.

Many Jews believed in Jesus, "Nevertheless even among the rulers many believed in Him, but because of the Pharisees they did not confess Him, lest they should be put out of the synagogue; for they loved the praise of men more than the praise of God." (John 12: 42, 43)

Although Pontius Pilate was aware of Jesus' innocence, he sentenced Jesus to death because he feared the people and feared for his position.

Herod killed the children of Bethlehem because He wanted to kill the "King" and secure his position. (Matt 3) Felix, Governor of Caesarea, was frightened when St. Paul talked about righteousness, self-control and the judgment to come. However, "Felix, wanting to do the Jews a favor, left Paul bound." (Acts 24: 27)

St. Pachomius, father of community says: "If someone honours you, you should grieve and not rejoice, because Paul and Barnabas tore their clothes when people praised them. Also Peter and the rest of the disciples were glad when they were whipped, because they were considered worthy to be humiliated for the sake of the Great Name."

He also says: "Eve yearned for the glory of divinity so she became naked of human glory. Similarly, whoever looks for praise from people, will be deprived of the glory of God."

How Can I Have True Dignity?

Through Possessing God Himself:

Christ is "Wisdom." Regarding this, Solomon the wise says: "I wisdom….riches and honor are with Me." (Prov. 8: 18) How wonderful and deep is this verse. It is true because Christ our Lord has riches and honor, "in Whom are hidden all the treasures of wisdom and knowledge." (Col. 2: 3) He who wants to gain true dignity, let him gain Christ first. Christ is a hidden treasure within us, but we do not feel His presence. (Matt. 13: 44)

My dear brethren, how honorable it is to have the Lord Jesus within you. It is honorable when you bear him like St. Mary. It is honorable when You feel His presence in your life because those who are with you will be more than those who are against you. (2 Malachi 6: 16) "For I will give you a mouth and wisdom which all your adversaries will not be able to contradict or resist." (Luke 21: 15)

The Lord honours his beloved ones, those who fear Him. The Apostle says; "…but glory, honour and peace to everyone who works what is good." (Rom. 2: 10)

The Lord highly honoured Saint John Chrysostom, Patriarch of Constantinople, because of his ascetic life, temperance, zeal and service. He gave him favour in the eyes of his people more than the king and queen. St. Paul says, "no man takes this honor to himself." (Heb. 5: 4)

Sometimes we feel that the world has forgotten the

children of God and has neglected them. However, the Lord reveals them to the world again, in the proper time, because they are the light of the world, the salt of the earth and the sweet aroma of Christ. Can the world live without light? Can the world live without the taste of salt? Can the world survive if the smell of sin spreads all over?

Life cannot be restored without the existence of saints and righteous people. Although they are a minority, they are needed, even though the world persecutes and humiliates them.

David was a young shepherd, forgotten by his father. However, the Lord took him out of the field and made him a king. John the Baptist disappeared into the wilderness, yet the Lord gave him honour and dignity, witnessing for him by saying,"Assuredly, I say to you, among those born of women there has not risen one greater than John the Baptist." (Matt.11: 11)

We need so much time to talk about the divine gifts that God gave to His saints. He gave them gifts of performing miracles, raising the dead, moving mountains, shutting lion mouths and enduring fire unharmed. Is there a better and more precious honor than this?

Blessed is the person who possesses God in his heart. For his heart will be a throne to His Creator and a pure temple for His dwelling.

THROUGH HUMILITY:

Solomon the Wise says, "By humility and the fear of the Lord, are riches and honor and life." (Prov. 22: 4)

The "honors" of the world are dreams and shadows that you can never reach. Your shadow will never remain under you unless you lie down completely on the ground. The same case with dignity. You will never acquire it except through humility. David the Prophet says, "My soul clings to the dust, revive me according to Your word." (Ps. 119: 25) Also, "The fear of the Lord is the instruction of wisdom, and before honour is humility." (Prov. 15: 33) Similarly, "Before destruction, the heart of a man is haughty, and before honor is humility." (Prov. 18: 12)

When the people asked John the Baptist if he was the Christ, John humbly replied: "whose sandal strap I am not worthy to loose." (Luke 3: 16) However, at the fullness of time, John was able to place his hand over the head of Christ and baptise Him in the River Jordan!

Now, see how the Lord "Raises the poor out of the dust, and lifts the needy out of the ash heap, that He may seat him with princes - with the princes of His people."

The Lord of Glory gained dignity and honour by tolerating humiliation and disgrace willingly. "Therefore God also has highly exalted Him and given Him the name which is above every name." (Phil. 2: 9)

Through Renouncing it:

If we give up the honour and praise of the world for the Lord's sake, He will love and honour us. St. Isaac says, "Give up the love of the world and God will love you. Don't look at the possessions of others and they will love you." He also says, "If you humiliate yourself so that people might honour you, the Lord will disclose it. However, if you honestly humiliate yourself and your deeds, God will direct the whole creation to honor you."

God said to Solomon, Son of David, King of Israel, "Because you have asked this thing, and have not asked long life for yourself, nor have asked riches for yourself, nor have asked the life of your enemies, but have asked for yourself understanding to discern justice, behold, I have done according to your words; see, I have given you a wise and understanding heart, so that there has not been anyone like you before you, nor shall any like you arise after you. And I have also given you what you have not asked: both riches and honor, so that there shall not be anyone like you among the kings all your days." (1 Kings 3: 11-13)

When the Lord saw that Solomon did not attach himself to the riches of the world, the Lord granted him riches, even though Solomon never asked. Furthermore, after experiencing these worldly riches, Solomon concluded:

"Vanity of vanities, all is vanity."

What profit has a man from all his labor

In which he toils under the sun?

One generation passes away,

and another generation comes;

But the earth abides forever.

The sun also rises, and the sun goes down,

And hastens to the place where it arose.

The wind goes toward the south,

And turns around to the north;

The wind whirls about continually,

And comes again on its circuit.

All the rivers run into the sea,

Yet the sea is not full;

To the place from which the rivers come,

There they return again. (Ecc. 1: 2-7)

Then where are "the rulers of this age, who are coming to nothing?" (1Cor. 2: 6) Where is Alexander the Great, Julius Caesar, Napoleon Bonaparte or Hitler? Where are they now? If you don't know the answer, go and ask the graves and the dust! However, the memory of the saints of God who renounced the pleasures of this world, are still alive. St Paul says about them, "….and through it, he being dead still speaks." (Heb. 11: 4) They are still performing miracles by their good reputation, their holy lives and their accepted intercession to the Lord.

Moses the Prophet despised the glory of Pharaoh and his palace, "esteeming the reproach of Christ greater riches than the treasures in Egypt." (Heb. 11: 26) As a result, God appointed him a leader of the children of Israel and "as God to Pharaoh" (Ex.7: 1)

Through Escaping it:

The saints gained dignity not by rest or hard toil, but by escaping it. St Isaac says, "He who seeks dignity will not find it, but he who escapes it knowledgably, dignity will follow him and guide people to where he is."

When you feel that the glories of the world are surrounding you and people are starting to praise you, just escape. When the Jews wanted to make the Lord Jesus their King, He fled and went alone to the mountain. (John 6: 15) The first Adam desired dignity. As a result, it was taken from him. The Second Adam – Lord Jesus- fled from dignity, "Therefore God also has highly exalted Him and given Him the name which is above every name," (Phil.2: 9)

History is a great witness in this matter: The saints who fled the world's praise, gained high honor from God as He preserved their names on earth and in heaven. When Constantine the Emperor heard about St. Anthony, he sent messengers asking him to bless his household and the Empire. St Moses the Black, who used to be the leader of a gang, was sought in the wilderness by a great ruler in Egypt who wanted to see him. St Sarabamoun the Veiled, Bishop of Menoufieh in the 20th century, used to be a laborer selling oil in the streets before his monasticism. Later, he was sought by the Governor of Cairo, Muhammed Ali Pasha, to heal his daughter who was demon possessed.

One of the best biographies in relation to this matter is the life of St. Mettaous, the 87th Pope, who is considered one of the greatest Popes of the See of St. Mark. When he was ordained a priest at the age of 18, he left his monastery and fled to St. Anthony's Monastery. There he did not mention that he was a priest, but served as a simple deacon. However, the honor which he fled from followed him and the Lord revealed it miraculously. While he was serving as a deacon in the Holy Liturgy, a hand came out of the Sanctuary and offered him incense three times during the reading of the Holy Gospel. When some of the elder monks saw it, they knew that he was a priest and informed him that he would be a Patriarch. Hearing this, he grieved a lot and left the Monastery heading to Jerusalem, where he worked as a slave. Honour followed him again and he became known when a monk came and complained to him about losing some money. He knew, by the Spirit, the place of the stolen money and returned it to the monk. Again, he fled to St. Anthony's Monastery then to St. Mary's Monastery in El Meharraq. When Pope Gabriel the 4th departed, the elders decided to nominate him for the Papacy, yet he escaped and boarded a ship to go to another country. The elders followed him, while he continued to escape. Finally he cut off the tip of his tongue to become mute, but the Lord who made Zachariah speak also made him speak. He yielded to become the Pope against his will.

Lots of similar stories about the saints show us that fleeing the honours and glories of the world is important if one wants to gain dignity.

The Life of Submission

"It is no longer I who live, but Christ lives in me." (Gal 2:20)

- The Most Accepted Offering
- Preparing for a Life of Submission
- Aspects of the Life of Submission
- Blessings of a Life of Submission
- How to live a Life of Submission?

The Most accepted Offering

In Christianity, Almsgiving is commendable and required. It is a commandment given by our Lord Jesus Christ Himself. St Paul addresses the priests in Ephesus and says: "I have shown you in every way, by laboring like this, that you must support the weak." Remember the words of the Lord Jesus, 'It is more blessed to give than to receive.' (Acts 20:35) We note that these words did not appear in the four Gospels, but were mentioned by St Paul and were known among the faithful. St Paul reminisces these words as he says, "Remember the words of the Lord Jesus." Being acknowledged among the faithful, implies that this was an agreed Christian principle.

It is nice to give the Lord material offerings; it is greater to present spiritual offerings, but better than these is a person who submits himself to the Lord. I do not mean offering ones life to consecration. However, submit your will and your whole life to God. When we give any offering, we give something of what we have but when we submit our will to the Will of God, we give ourselves TOTALLY to the Lord, and the Lord accepts this as a living offering.

When I give to the poor or give monetary donations to the church, I am offering part of my wealth and not all of it. If I serve the Lord honestly, I am offering part of my time and not all of it. When I labor for a spiritual matter, I am offering part of my effort and not all of it.

However, a life of submission means submitting one's whole life to God. Consequently, all of one's efforts, behaviour, thoughts or actions are according to the will of God. St Paul puts it: "It is no longer I who live, but Christ lives in me." (Gal 2:20)

Submission is very clear in the life of the Lord Jesus for He said: "I have come down from heaven, not to do My own will, but the will of Him who sent Me." (John 6:38) In his prayer in Gethsemane, He addresses the Father: "If it is possible, let this cup pass from Me; nevertheless, not as I will, but as You will." (Matt 26:39) When the disciples asked Him to teach them how to pray, He taught them the best prayer: "When you pray say our Father who art in heaven… Your will be done on earth as it is in heaven…" This teaches us to have the Will of God active in our lives, just as it is in Heaven. In Heaven, nothing can obstruct the Will of God, but unfortunately man on earth obstructs the Will of God through their own free will. St Peter also stresses the virtue of Submission in the life of Jesus Christ: "Who, when He was reviled, did not revile in return; when He suffered, He did not threaten, but committed Himself to Him who judges righteously." (1 Peter 2:23)

PREPARING FOR A LIFE OF SUBMISSION

The life of submission is not easy, but quite difficult as it deals with one's personal desires, the mind and the ego. There are three important elements one must consider before practicing submission.

To be void of all desires:

A person who has desires cannot submit his life to God. Even if he tries, it will not be a total submission. For this reason, whoever wants to submit his life to God must be void of all desires, even those regarding spiritual matters. The purpose of any spiritual matter is to be united with God but the way to reach this goal must be left to God's will.

Humility

One cannot live a life of submission without humility, for a person who is sure of himself and his ability in managing his own life, cannot submit to God in simple faith. He would analyse his relationship with God, according to his own mind and will accept what he likes and refuse what he dislikes.

This person may misinterpret certain events in his life as evil which were meant for his good. His mind may acknowledge some matters as proper which are not. His belief in himself makes it difficult to submit his life to God.

Faith:

No one can submit his life to God unless he believes that God can take care of him and manage all his affairs. He should believe that whatever God does is done wisely and that he does not need to interfere. If that person doubts God's love and care, how can he live a life of submission? Faith in God is a total trust in Him.

Aspects of the Life of Submission

Although submission is an inner way of life, it also possesses visible attributes that can be seen:

Submission of one's own will means the person will agree with the will of God. In other words, a person becomes like a melted candle that can accept any picture printed on it. He cannot live a life of submission and other times do his own will. This is very clear in what Saul (St. Paul) says: "Lord, what do you want me to do?" (Acts 9:6) These words express total submission. Consequently, it was the turning point in the life of this great apostle, who lived the rest of his life being led by the Holy Spirit. This is clear in some of his sayings: "I have been crucified with Christ; it is no longer I who live, but Christ lives in me; and the life which I now live in the flesh I live by faith in the Son of God, who loved me and gave Himself for me." (Gal 2:20); "And see, now I go bound in the spirit to Jerusalem, not knowing the things that will happen to me there, except that the Holy Spirit testifies in every city, saying that chains and tribulations await me. But none of these things move me; nor do I count my life dear to myself, so that I may finish my race with joy, and the ministry which I received from the Lord Jesus, to testify to the gospel of the grace of God." (Acts 20:22-24). He lived in total obedience to the Holy Spirit, though he knew that chains and tribulations awaited him. This is the life of submission.

b) One's thoughts become the thoughts of God. St Paul says: "We have the mind of Christ." (1 Cor 2:16) This is a natural outcome of a life of submission, for if a person totally submits his life to God, then God will direct his thoughts. The Psalmist says: "I was so foolish and ignorant...Nevertheless I am continually with You; You hold me by my right hand. You will guide me with Your counsel." (Psalm 73:22-24)

All the actions of a person will be according to God's will. It is written about David the Prophet and King: "I have found David, the son of Jesse, a man after My own heart, who will do all My will." (Acts 13:22) David deserved this testimony as he lived a life of submission and always said: "My heart is steadfast, O God, my heart is steadfast." (Psalm 57:7) This means, David was ready to obey God totally and to submit to His will wholeheartedly.

The person is calm, no matter what the event. If something unexpected occurs and the person is upset, then he/she is not totally submissive to God. A submissive person will be calm in any circumstance and thankful in any event because he believes that it is God's will and for his own good.

BLESSINGS OF THE LIFE OF SUBMISSION

What can a person gain from a life of submission to God? What are the blessings?

A constant joy and a continuous peace that is not disturbed by fear or anxiety. The Psalmist says: "I delight to do Your will, O my God," (Psalm 40:8); "But let all those rejoice who put their trust in You; let them ever shout for joy, because You defend them; Let those also who love Your name be joyful in You." (Psalm 5:11). Also joy is a fruit of the Spirit (Gal 5:22) while sadness is a fruit of sin.

The reason for this inner joy and peace is the result of doing God's will and the faith that follows, "... all things work together for good to those who love God." (Rom 8:28) Moreover, the wise man says: "No grave trouble will overtake the righteous." (Proverbs 12:21)

Just because a person submits to God totally, does not mean he will not face hardships; it may be on the contrary: "Many are the afflictions of the righteous, but the Lord delivers him out of them all." (Psalm 34:19). In a way, he is like the three men in the fiery furnace in Babylon, who were walking in the furnace and the fire did not even burn a hair from their heads; it only burnt their chains, allowing them to walk freely in the furnace. The secret was that a fourth one was with them who looked like the Son of God. (Daniel 3) This is our God who: "In all their affliction, He was afflicted, and the Angel of His Presence saved them." (Is 63:9)

Complete calmness. If a person knows how to submit his will to God's will, then he will be calm and nothing will disturb him, for he gave his life to God who "For of Him and through Him and to Him are all things." (Rom 11:36) He always feels that his life is in God's hand who cares for him, loves him and can deliver him from any trouble. David's psalms are full of these feelings: "Though I walk through the valley of the shadow of death, I will fear no evil; For You are with me; Your rod and Your staff, they comfort me." (Psalm 23:4); "The LORD is my light and my salvation; Whom shall I fear? The LORD is the strength of my life; Of whom shall I be afraid? My enemies and foes, they stumbled and fell. Though an army may encamp against me, My heart shall not fear" (Psalm 27); "God is our refuge and strength, a very present help in trouble. Therefore we will not fear even though the earth be removed, and though the mountains be carried into the midst of the sea." (Psalm 46)

A person who submits to God will feel calmness because he knows that God will only do good, just as St Paul says: "All things work together for good to those who love God." (Rom 8:28) Even if an unexpected event occurs, he still believes that there is something good behind it.

There is a story about a saint who lived a life of submission. On his trip to Alexander, some atheists gathered around him, cursing and abusing him, while he maintained a calm attitude. One of them asked him: "Tell us what sort of miracles did this Nazarene whom you believe in do?" The saint answered: "One of His miracles is this: that you are cursing and abusing me while I am content and joyful."

There was another saintly monk who performed miracles yet did not work or strive hard. When the Abbot of the monastery noticed this, he questioned him regarding his affairs. This monk replied that although he did not pray or fast more than the other monks, he was never upset about anything. The Abbot asked him: "Weren't you disturbed when the enemies raided the monastery and burnt the grain store?" The monk said: "I trained myself to accept everything that happens and to thankfully submit to God." The Abbot realised that the monk's ability to perform miracles was a result of his calmness and his life of submission.

Humility is needed before a life of submission can be sought. Parallel to this, a life of submission increases one's meekness, a foundation of spirituality.

You receive an assurance regarding the final judgment. By submitting one's life to God, you know you cannot be judged for doing His will. Every Christian strives hard spiritually so as not to be judged in the final day. If submitting one's life to God will protect me from Judgment, then what more can one desire?

Through a life of submission, God becomes our Protector, as the Psalmist says: "Because he has set his love upon Me, therefore I will deliver him; I will set him on high, because he has known My name. He shall call upon Me, and I will answer him; I will be with him in trouble; I will deliver him and honor him. With long life I will satisfy him, and show him My salvation."(Psalm 91)

A Life of submission will increase our love for God.

Love cannot be complete unless our will is similar to God's will. "If you love Me, keep My commandments." (John 14:15)

Submission will help us acquire other spiritual virtues like obedience, patience and tolerance. The interference of my will can be an obstacle which may prevent me from obtaining these virtues. If a person is not submissive to God, he cannot be obedient. By being obedient in matters that do not appear to be in one's favour, one practices patience, which leads to tolerance (Rom 5:4).

The life of submission will allow us to experience a holy life with God. God created man free and through this freedom man failed to receive many blessings because Man's will was not the same as God's will. The Lord Jesus says to the people in Jerusalem: "How often I wanted to gather your children together ... but you were not willing! See! Your house is left to you desolate." (Matt 23:37,38)

How to live a Life of Submission?

Firstly, One should convince himself that nothing happens to him or to the world, unless it is God's will and unless it is taken from His permission. When Peter, having a sword, drew it and struck the high priest's servant, and cut off his right ear, Jesus said to Peter, "Put your sword into the sheath. Shall I not drink the cup which My Father has given Me?"(John 18:11) The Lord did not say: The cup that Judas and the high priests have given Me but the Father Almighty. Furthermore, Pilate said to Jesus, "Do You not know that I have power to crucify You, and power to release You?" Jesus answered, "You could have no power at all against Me unless it had been given you from above." (John 19:10,11)

King Herod wanted to kill the Lord Jesus when He was a child and so he killed all the children in Bethlehem who were two years and under, but he could not fulfill his murderous intent as it was not yet the hour for Jesus to be killed. (Matt 2:16) Many times the Jews wanted to kill Jesus and one time they took Him out of their city to throw Him down over the cliff. "Then passing through the midst of them, He went His way." (Luke 4:30) However, when His hour came, that which was appointed from eternity, He said to those who came to arrest Him: "... this is your hour, and the power of darkness." (Luke 22:53)

How many times did King Saul try to kill David but failed in all his attempts? This is because "God did not deliver him into his hand." (1 Sam 23:14) Joseph's brothers wanted to get rid of him but the Lord sent him to Egypt to preserve lives. Later, Joseph told his brothers in Egypt: "But now, do not therefore be grieved or angry with yourselves because you sold me here; for God sent me before you to preserve lives. ...And God sent me before you to preserve a posterity for you in the earth, and to save your lives by a great deliverance. So now it was not you who sent me here, but God." (Gen 45:5-8) He also told them: "Do not be afraid... you meant evil against me; but God meant it for good." (Gen 50:19,20)

What a great feeling that our lives are in God's loving and almighty Hand. If we feel this way, we will gladly and willingly submit ourselves to God. St Cyprian commented on "Lead us not into temptation" by saying: "We address God, not Satan, so we are not led into temptation." This is how the saints understood the life of submission. The devil used to appear in front of St Anthony in many different forms of wild beasts. The Saint used to tell the devil: "If you have any authority on me, one of you would have been enough to fight a man like myself, but God took away your strength."

Secondly, When unexpected or unwanted events occur, one should never be upset, but should ask God to amend whatever is lacking in himself. While in the desert, the Jews hated eating the manna and longed for meat so God gave them meat abundantly. He gave them their desire but this had an evil result: "So they ate and were well filled, for He gave them their own desire. They were not deprived of their craving; but while their food was still in their mouths, the wrath of God came against them, and slew the stoutest of them, and struck down the choice men of Israel." (Psalm 78:29-31) It would have been better for the Israelites to appreciate the manna and thank God for all His gifts in this secluded desert!

The Principle of the Narrow Gate

"Enter by the narrow gate; for wide is the gate and broad is the way that leads to destruction"

(Luke 13:23-27)

- What is the narrow gate?
- The principle of the narrow gate in spiritual practices
- What did the Fathers say?
- The principle of the narrow gate in problems in life

What is the Narrow Gate?

When someone asked the Lord Jesus, "Lord, are there few who are saved?" He said to them, "Strive to enter through the narrow gate, for many, I say to you, will seek to enter and will not be able. When once the Master of the house has risen up and shut the door, and you begin to stand outside and knock at the door, saying, 'Lord, Lord, open for us,' and He will answer and say to you, 'I do not know you, where are you from,' then you will begin to say, 'We ate and drank in Your presence, and You taught in our streets.' But He will say, 'I tell you I do not know you, where are you from. Depart from Me, all you workers of iniquity.' (Luke 13:23-27)

Moreover, in His Sermon on the Mount, the Lord Jesus said: "Enter by the narrow gate; for wide is the gate and broad is the way that leads to destruction, and there are many who go in by it. Because narrow is the gate and difficult is the way which leads to life, and there are few who find it." (Matt 7:13,14)

The "narrow gate" and the "difficult way" is a voluntary choice where one must put limitations on their daily life, while accepting hardships and pressures patiently, gladly and thankfully. The Lord Christ refers to this difficult way when He tells us to carry our Cross.

In the first part of the book we talked at length about God's ultimate love. Here we question: Is there a contradiction between the great love of God towards man, because by His permission we face troubles and pains, and are asked to voluntarily enter through the narrow gate and carry the Cross?

The Lord Jesus mentioned on several occasions that His children and all who believe in Him will face many kinds of troubles. In addition, He made carrying the Cross a condition of Christian discipleship. He said: "I will send you as lambs among wolves." (Luke 10:3); "In the world you will have tribulation."(John 16:33); "The time is coming that whoever kills you will think that he offers God service." (John 16:2) "You will be hated by all for My name's sake." (Matt 10:22); "You will weep and lament, but the world will rejoice." (John 16:20)

The question that comes to mind is: How can this invitation to accept hardships be in agreement with God's love? In other words: If God really loves us, is He bothered by our troubles?!

The answer to this question is in Isaiah's words about the Lord: "In all their affliction He was afflicted, and the Angel of His Presence saved them." (Is 63:9) This means that God is concerned in our troubles. If this is the case, then why does He permit it while He can prevent it?! There must be a certain Godly wisdom for these troubles; otherwise God would not permit it.

The troubles that a person experiences are for their own good, and they coincide with God's love and His goodness. The Lord said: "The very hairs of your head are all numbered." (Matt 10:30; Luke 12:7). Through Isaiah He said: "See, I have inscribed you on the palms of My hands;" (Is 49:16). Also through Zechariah He said: "For thus says the Lord of hosts: ...for he who touches you touches the apple of His eye." (Zech 2:8)

At the beginning of Christianity, believing in Jesus Christ was the start of troubles and hardships as many faced martyrdom and death. "All who desire to live godly in Christ Jesus will suffer persecution." (2 Tim 3:12) In spite of this, the Christian faith spread all over the world and Christians preferred to live with Jesus, accepting pain and hardships rather than denying Him for the pleasures of the world and its passing glory. There must then be a motive behind hardships and pains, for the martyrs and confessors were not that naïve to bear terrible pains for no cost!! The motive was the blessings.

So, what is the wisdom behind the narrow gate?

It is the commandment of Jesus and His way:

We previously mentioned the commandment of Jesus Christ and how he calls us all to enter by the narrow gate. The narrow gate is the way of the Cross. The Lord Jesus walked that way with His blessed feet. It is the way from Bethlehem to Golgotha. So, if the narrow way is the way of the Cross, then hardships are carrying the Cross. What did the Lord say about this?

"And he who does not take his cross and follow after Me is not worthy of Me." (Matt 10:38) "And whoever does not bear his cross and come after Me cannot be My disciple." (Luke 14:27) "If anyone desires to come after Me, let him deny himself, and take up his cross, and follow Me." (Matt 16:24; Mark 8:34)

Some may think that these commandments were just

for the disciples and apostles of the Lord but St Luke in his Gospel clarified that these commandments are for everyone: "Then He said to them all, "If anyone desires to come after Me, let him deny himself, and take up his cross daily, and follow Me." (Luke 9:23) The same was said to the rich man who asked Jesus about what to do to inherit eternal life. The Lord's reply was: "Go your way, sell whatever you have and give to the poor, and you will have treasure in heaven; and come, take up the cross, and follow Me." (Mark 10:21) It is clear that following the Lord Jesus involves carrying a cross, which means accepting hardships and enduring suffering gladly.

Jesus faced the narrow gate since His birth as a man; He faced the difficult way from Bethlehem to Golgotha. His birth was in a manger, then He escaped to Egypt to flee from Herod who wanted to kill Him. He faced the challenges of the Jews who fought Him during His missionary period for more than three years. During that time, He endured curses and insults from His creation. He endured the betrayal of Judas and accepted suffering with His own will for the salvation of humanity. These are features of the narrow gate that the Lord Jesus entered with His free will in His humanity.

<u>We imitate Jesus:</u>

Jesus Christ is our example. We want to imitate Him and follow in His steps, "Christ also suffered for us, leaving us an example, that you should follow His steps." (1 Peter 2:21) We are supposed "to be conformed to the image of His Son, that He might be the firstborn among many brethren." (Rom 8:29) What is the image of the Son of God except that of holiness and suffering. "He is despised and rejected by men, A Man of sorrows and acquainted with grief." (Is 53:3)

The Lord Jesus loved suffering, "But I have a baptism to be baptized with, and how distressed I am till it is accomplished!" (Luke 12:50) St Paul says about Him "who for the joy that was set before Him endured the cross, despising the shame." (Heb 12:2) The Lord Jesus asked James and John, Zebedee's sons: "Are you able to drink the cup that I am about to drink, and be baptized with the baptism that I am baptized with?" They said to Him, "We are able." (Matt 20:22)

One of the fathers said: "Gladness in suffering is the measure of the love of Christ. A loving person will welcome suffering and be glad while a lukewarm person will escape from it and be upset by it. The Lord Jesus proved His love to humanity by His suffering; it is then proper and just that humans show their true love by suffering for Him." This is what St Paul meant when he wrote to the Romans commanding them "Present your bodies a living sacrifice, holy, acceptable to God." (Rom 12:1)

It is the way of all saints:

The Lord Jesus said: "He who does not take his cross and follow after Me is not worthy of Me. Whoever does not bear his cross and come after Me cannot be My disciple." (Matt 10:38; Luke 14:27) All holy people walked the difficult way and entered by the narrow gate. All holy people carried a cross. Carrying a cross is a condition that must be met before one can become the Lord's disciple.

The apostles, who were the early believers in the New Testament, entered by the narrow gate, as did their Master who carried the cross gladly. St James says: "My brethren, count it all joy when you fall into various trials, knowing that the testing of your faith produces patience. But let patience have its perfect work, that you may be perfect and complete, lacking nothing." (James 1:2-4) St Peter tells the believers: "If you should suffer for righteousness' sake, you are blessed...since Christ suffered for us in the flesh, arm yourselves also with the same mind...but rejoice to the extent that you partake of Christ's sufferings, that when His glory is revealed, you may also be glad with exceeding joy." (1 Peter 3:14, 4:1, 13)

In the opening of Revelation, St John says to the believers: "I, John, both your brother and companion in the tribulation and kingdom and patience of Jesus Christ." (Rev 1:9) It is clear here that tribulation and kingdom go hand in hand.

When we mention St Paul and his conversion to Christianity, we notice that the Lord Jesus appeared and spoke to Ananias the Bishop of Damascus who later baptised St Paul, "For I will show him how many things he must suffer for My name's sake." (Acts 9:16) We notice here that these words were not a threat or punishment to St Paul for his previous persecution of the church, but these were a prediction of the blessings he will encounter through his sufferings in his service.

Isn't it strange that suffering is considered a blessing? At one point, Peter told the Lord, "See, we have left all and followed You." So Jesus answered and said, "Assuredly, I say to you, there is no one who has left house or brothers or sisters or father or mother or wife or children or lands, for My sake and the gospel's, who shall not receive a hundredfold now in this time—houses and brothers and sisters and mothers and children and lands, with persecutions—and in the age to come, eternal life." (Mark 10:28-30) You see how Jesus counts persecutions as blessings?!

St. Paul wrote a lot about how sufferings and hardships are accompanied with blessings:

He considered it a fellowship with Jesus in His suffering: "That I may know Him and the power of His resurrection, and the fellowship of His sufferings, being conformed to His death." (Php 3:10)

He rejoices in hardships, "I now rejoice in my sufferings for you, and fill up in my flesh what is lacking in the afflictions of Christ, for the sake of His Body, which is the church." (Col 1:24) This is a remarkable expression where St Paul describes the believers as the secret unseen body of Christ who, when they suffer, fill up what is lacking in the afflictions of Christ. When Jesus on the cross said "It is finished," He was talking about the salvation of humanity, which was finished by His Death on the cross, but His suffering and afflictions are not finished yet. The believers will fill it up by their endurance of whatever comes their way for the sake of Jesus and their belief.

St. Paul reveals that afflictions are our permit to the eternal kingdom. He was encouraging the believers in Asia Minor saying: "We must through many tribulations enter the kingdom of God." (Acts 14:22) "For you yourselves know that we are appointed to this. For, in fact, we told you before when we were with you that we would suffer tribulation." (1 Thess 3:2-4)

Moreover, St Paul surpasses the stage of enduring patiently to praising it, "And not only that, but we also glory in tribulations, knowing that tribulation produces perseverance; and perseverance, character; and character, hope." (Rom 5:3,4) He also rejoices in it, "Therefore I take pleasure in infirmities, in reproaches, in needs, in persecutions, in distresses, for Christ's sake. For when I am weak, then I am strong." (2 Cor 12:10) In afflictions, the Grace of God is manifested, consoling man as he is in partnership with the Lord in His suffering. The apostle even elevates tribulations as they are a spiritual gift from God to man: "For to you it has been granted on behalf of Christ, not only to believe in Him, but also to suffer for His sake." (Phil 1:29)

If we move from the apostles of Christ to the saints in general, we find that all agree on the blessings of the narrow gate and the difficult way. The sayings of the saints express their personal experience.

- St. Paul the Simple, the disciple of St Anthony the Great said: "Whoever escapes from trouble, God escapes from him."

- In his final sermon, St Macarius the Great said to his sons, the monks: "Who was crowned without labor; who became rich without working; who won without laboring first; who was lazy and gathered wealth; and who was idle and did not lose his fortune? It is with numerous sufferings we would enter the heavenly kingdom. Let each one of you be careful to accept hardships gladly knowing that behind it there is richness and rest."

- St. Pachomius, the father of community said:

"Accept temptations with joy, realizing the glory that follows. If you are certain about this, you will be able to bear it and even ask God not to take it away." He also says: "Do you think that cutting limbs and burning are the only martyrdom? No. It is the pain of tolerating the beating of devils and accepting sickness with thanksgiving. This is martyrdom. Why would St Paul write that he is dying every day? He was not literally dying but tolerating with patience whatever comes his way."

- St. Isaac the Syrian said:"Do not despise hardships, for enduring it will lead to honor and through it you draw near the Lord. The righteous accepts adversity with joy."

- St. Barsanuphius says: "Why do you act childishly in difficult situations just like a worldly human being? Don't you know that pain is for the saints? Haven't you heard that many are the afflictions of the righteous and from all of it God will save them? Don't you know that the righteous will be tested by suffering just like the gold is tested by fire. So if we are righteous, we will be tested by suffering and if we are sinners, we will be chastened by suffering."

- One of the fathers said: "If a person endures a difficulty for the sake of God, God will consider him a martyr for the tears he shed. Those tears take place of the shedding of blood."

<u>It is the manner that suits a person spiritually:</u>

If God allows trials for man, this does not mean that God enjoys looking at man suffer. On the contrary, God wants spiritual goodness for man and because He knows the nature of man and his tendency towards the earthly and bodily desires, God deals with him in a suitable way. When God drowned the world with the flood, Noah left the ark, built an altar to God and the LORD smelled a soothing aroma. Then the LORD said in His heart, "I will never again curse the ground for man's sake, although the imagination of man's heart is evil from his youth; nor will I again destroy every living thing as I have done." (Gen 8:20-21)

St. Paul said: "Walk in the Spirit, and you shall not fulfill the lust of the flesh. For the flesh lusts against the Spirit, and the Spirit against the flesh; and these are contrary to one another, so that you do not do the things that you wish." (Gal 5:16-17) St Paul also mentions how the nature of man bends towards evil: "For I know that in me (that is, in my flesh) nothing good dwells; for to will is present with me, but how to perform what is good I do not find. For the good that I will to do, I do not do; but the evil I will not to do, that I practice. Now if I do what I will not to do, it is no longer I who do it, but sin that dwells in me. I find then a law, that evil is present with me, the one who wills to do good. For I delight in the law of God according to the inward man. But I see another law in my members, warring against the law of my mind, and bringing me into captivity to the law of sin which is in my members. O wretched man that I am! Who will deliver me from this body of death?" (Rom 7:18-24)

Thus we see that man is weak according to his nature and there are many attractive desires that push him towards what is earthly and bodily. Therefore, troubles are useful to man as they alert him to return to the right path. It makes man realise his weak nature so that he may raise his mind and heart to ask for help. The Psalmist says: "My support is from the Lord." (Psalm 18:18)

David the Prophet said: "Now in my prosperity I said, "I shall never be moved." LORD, by Your favor You have made my mountain stand strong; You hid Your face, and I was troubled." (Psalm 30:6-7) David says that with God, he is strong and shall not be moved, but if God hides His face, he will grow worried and terrified. He continues saying: "I cried out to You, O LORD; and to the LORD I made supplication: Hear, O LORD, and have mercy on me; LORD, be my helper!" You have turned for me my mourning into dancing; You have put off my sackcloth and clothed me with gladness."

Man is quite weak, and his will often betrays him, even though he knows what is right. Only by the Grace of God do we have support. Without it, we could be in such a bad situation. God deals differently with each one according to each one's nature and for his good. Sadly man only pays attention through suffering. Someone said: "Trouble is God's language to His beloved!!" Thus, suffering is beneficial for man's salvation.

Furthermore, through sufferings, God cleanses man from his sins and weaknesses. The Lord Jesus Christ says: "I am the true vine, and My Father is the vinedresser. Every branch in Me that does not bear fruit He takes away; and every branch that bears fruit He prunes, that it may bear more fruit." (John 15:1-2) Pruning involves cutting parts off the branches and if plants could talk, they would express their pain! In some plants, when they are cut, there is a sort of liquid that comes out as if it were tears! This is what God does to His beloved children. He prunes them so that they produce more spiritual fruits. One of the fathers said: "When a branch is pruned, liquid seeps out, as if it is weeping, but later on, its buds start to appear and they bear beautiful flowers and delicious fruits. Similarly, a Christian is the secret branch of Jesus, the True Vine. Jesus initially appears to squash him, which causes pain, but later he is renewed and the fruits of the Holy Spirit multiply in him." St Augustine says: "The straw and the wheat are different things but the threshing machine passes over both, crushing the straw and cleaning the wheat."

<u>It is the way to eternal glory:</u>

The Book of Acts mentions St Paul and St Barnabas while they were in cities of Asia Minor. They were "strengthening the souls of the disciples, exhorting them to continue in the faith, and saying, "We must through many tribulations enter the kingdom of God."" (Acts 14:22) The word "must" shows the necessity of many tribulations.

The Thessalonians showed their willingness to accept the Christian faith. Consequently, their faith increased and their virtues flourished. So St Paul wrote to them, encouraging them and explaining that accepting persecutions and tribulations is an indication that they are worthy of the kingdom of God. "We ourselves boast of you among the churches of God for your patience and faith in all your persecutions and tribulations that you endure, which is manifest evidence of the righteous judgment of God, that you may be counted worthy of the kingdom of God, for which you also suffer; since it is a righteous thing with God to repay with tribulation those who trouble you, and to give you who are troubled rest with us when the Lord Jesus is revealed from heaven with His mighty angels." (2 Thess 1:3-7) He also writes to the Corinthians: "For our light affliction, which is but for a moment, is working for us a far more exceeding and eternal weight of glory." (2 Cor 4:17)

In Revelations, St John the Apostle describes the place of those who tolerate sufferings in the other world: "After these things I looked, and behold, a great multitude which no one could number, of all nations, tribes, peoples, and tongues, standing before the throne and before the Lamb, clothed with white robes, with palm branches in their hands, and crying out with a loud voice, saying, "Salvation belongs to our God who sits on the throne, and to the Lamb!" All the angels stood around the throne and the elders and the four living creatures, and fell on their faces before the throne and worshiped God saying: "Amen! Blessing and glory and wisdom, thanksgiving and honor and power and might, Be to our God forever and ever. Amen." Then one of the elders answered, saying to me, "Who are these arrayed in white robes, and where did they come from?" And I said to him, "Sir, you know." So he said to me, "These are the ones who come out of the great tribulation, and washed their robes and made them white in the blood of the Lamb. Therefore they are before the throne of God, and serve Him day and night in His temple. And He who sits on the throne will dwell among them. They shall neither hunger anymore nor thirst anymore; the sun shall not strike them, nor any heat; for the Lamb who is in the midst of the throne will shepherd them and lead them to living fountains of waters. And God will wipe away every tear from their eyes." (Rev 7:9-17)

Pain and suffering prepare us for eternal happiness. This is what the Lord revealed to His disciples saying: "Most assuredly, I say to you that you will weep and lament, but the world will rejoice; and you will be sorrowful, but your sorrow will be turned into joy." (John 16:20)

The Principle of the Narrow Gate in Our Spiritual Practices

The narrow gate principle not only applies in troubles and pressures that man faces; it also includes what man does by choice in his spiritual struggle. We will demonstrate some examples of the narrow gate in one's spiritual life.

First: In Repentance

Without a doubt, repentance is a narrow gate that a man enters by choice. For in repentance a person must not give in to whatever he wishes, especially unholy desires. We should understand the Lord's commandment: "Strive to enter by the narrow gate," which means it is a voluntary action from man.

St John Saba says: "Just like Adam had sons from Eve, Jesus is the true Father and through baptism and repentance, we become His sons. Repentance is a narrow gate and whoever is patient in its dark difficulty, will enjoy the kingdom of light when he gets out. It is the gate to life. Who can see the face of God without repentance and hope? Who was not cleansed without it? Repentance delivered David from his sin and Nineveh was saved by it."

DIFFICULTY OF REPENTANCE:

<u>Difficulty to leave loved lusts:</u>

In any good work, we should not deny the Grace of God as the Lord Jesus said: "Without Me, you can do nothing." (John 15:5); "No one can come to Me unless the Father who sent Me draws him." (John 6:44)

Thus repentance needs the Grace of God and that is why Jeremiah cried to the Lord saying: "Restore me, and I will return, for You are the LORD my God." (Jer 31:18) However, one must not deny his role in repentance. He must struggle to stop his sins and he must have a willingness to live with God. Here we remember St Augustine's famous saying: "God who created you without you, will not save you without you." This means that you did not participate in your creation but when it comes to your salvation, you have a role and a work to do. The Grace of God will not save you if you are passive and not making any effort to repent.

There are many things that a person loves and sometimes becomes a slave to. In this case, one needs to be strong. One needs to struggle and trust in God's support. He must trust in himself too. One should put the world on one side of the scale and Jesus' love and glory on the other side. One should then choose Barabbas or Jesus (Matt 27:17) Barabbas was a symbol of the existing world, so do not be like the Jews who chose Barabbas in front of Pontius Pilate.

I do not know which lust or desire you are struggling with as there are many types. But I am reminding you of Jesus' commandment to love Him with all your heart, with all your thought, with all your soul and with all your ability. He who loves father or mother, a son or daughter, more than Me, is not worthy of Me. (Matt 10:37) Loving parents and children is a legitimate and holy love, yet God should be loved above all. I remind you of the Almighty God's words: "And he who does not take his cross and follow after Me is not worthy of Me. He who finds his life will lose it, and he who loses his life for My sake will find it." (Matt 10:38-39)

Listen to what I am saying...if you want to live for God with all your heart, He will give you the strength and victory because "All things are possible to him who believes;" (Mark 9:23) "I can do all things through Christ who strengthens me." (Phil 4:13) A child is weaned from his mother's milk with difficulty but he cannot grow up without weaning and gradually eating grown up food.

Struggle is a necessity in all stages of man's life, for spiritual warfare changes into different forms, as one grows up. However, with God's grace and constant struggle, we will be able to conquer. The great St. Paul says: "Everyone who competes for the prize is temperate in all things... But I discipline my body and bring it into subjection, lest, when I have preached to others, I myself should become disqualified." (1 Cor 9:27) What is this St Paul? You are worried that you may be disqualified after all the services you did? You are worried that you may be disqualified by the hardships of missionary work and your personal heavenly visions? He also wrote to the Hebrews saying: "You have not yet resisted to bloodshed, striving against sin." (Heb 12:4) If this is the standard of the great apostle in struggle, what can we do?!

Difficulty in leaving bad friendships

Friendship is a very critical aspect in once life, for it has a big influence on a person and that is what St Paul says: "Do not be deceived. Evil company corrupts good habits." (1 Cor 15:33) An unclean hand will dirty anything it touches, just like a bad friendship. On the contrary, a good friendship is a blessing and a great support to a person in his spiritual life. A person may have a friend since childhood, the innocence age, but when this friend grows up, he may deviate from the right path. If this friendship continues, it is possible that the other person will be affected and change for the worse too.

Man, by nature, turns to evil and thus the Holy Bible advises us to escape from sin and evil. This is what happened to Lot, who lived in Sodom and Gomorrah. The angel told him, "Escape for your life! Do not look behind you nor stay anywhere in the plain. Escape to the mountains, lest you be destroyed." (Gen 19:17) The angel warned him not to look back so that he may not desire anything in the city; He also warned him not to stay anywhere near that area.

Difficulty in stopping evil habits

Any habit becomes one if it is practiced for a period of time. It is just like a tree. A small tree can be easily uprooted from the ground, but it is quite hard to uproot if its roots have penetrated the earth over a passage of time.

However, if one has a bad habit, it is not impossible to change, as the apostle says: "I can do all things through Christ who strengthens me." (Php 4:13) If the Lord is able to move mountains and perform miracles, he can surely help a person overcome a bad habit.

We cannot mention all bad habits here, but surely they are known to everyone. We will not discuss bad habits related to sexual behaviour but we will mention some bad habits that are not considered as such by many, such as smoking, drinking alcohol (even in small amounts) or drinking tea and coffee. It is dangerous for any habit to take hold of a person. For instance, it is dangerous for someone to be addicted to tea and coffee. Without which they cannot function properly or think well. Such a habit can obstruct a person from certain spiritual practices such as fasting. Those people who are used to drinking something as soon as they wake up, may not be able to enjoy the blessings of fasting.

An evil habit can enslave a person and he may not be free as God made us. Jesus came to free us from all bondages, "Therefore if the Son makes you free, you shall be free indeed." (John 8:36)

If you feel you are free in Jesus, then take care not to be bound by anything. Be careful. Before saying, "I can do all things through Christ who strengthen me," St Paul says: "I have learned in whatever state I am, to be content: I know how to be abased, and I know how to abound. Everywhere and in all things I have learned both to be full and to be hungry, both to abound and to suffer need." (Phil 4:11,12)

Remembering old sins:

This is one of the difficulties of repentance for the evil one reminds a person of his old sins and may use it to make him think again in an unholy manner.

The church prays for this in the reconciliation prayer in the Holy Liturgy and asks God to purify us from every lust, every deceit and the remembrance of every evil entailing death. This is true because if a person is dragged into thinking of a past sin, he may be attracted to the desire again.

To overcome this, a person needs will power, struggle and patience. He must not fear spiritual enemies or feel his weakness. We are nothing without God and if we feel the presence of God near us, let us say: "If God is for us, who can be against us?" (Rom 8:31); "I can do all things through Christ who strengthens me." (Phil 4:13)

Second: In the practices of prayer, fasting and holy readings.

By discussing the narrow path of repentance, we are talking about the negatives of sin and bad habits. However, there are many positives in the spiritual life that we need. Positives are important in a person's spiritual life just like the spirit of man. The most important positives are prayer, fasting and holy readings. We will not be able to discuss these in detail but will approach them in relation to the narrow gate.

The saintly fathers recommended compulsion. They derived this from the teachings of the Lord Jesus when He says: "The kingdom of heaven suffers violence, and the violent take it by force." (Matt 11:12) This is not easy but everything in life is reached through hard work and great effort especially if what we are trying to achieve is precious. A student, a farmer or a laborer does not succeed except by working hard. How about heaven? If a student studies hard and sleeps less to gain his certificate, then heaven also deserves from us lots of hard work!

We read about how the Lord Jesus Christ spent all night in prayer. The Holy One who did not need prayers, prayed deeply and constantly. We are often deceived by our bodies and feel we are weak and tired. If we respond to this feeling, we will stop any spiritual practice.

Third: In Confession

Without a doubt, confessing our sins in front of the priest is definitely a narrow gate that we all must enter. Many people are ashamed to confess their sins, but it is through this holy sacrament that we obtain forgiveness. One must deny their selves and stand strong in front of this narrow gate.

Though embarrassment is hard, these feelings are useful for repentance. It is important to feel the pain of sin in confession, just like we feel the pleasure of sin as we commit it. One of the fathers said that the sacrament of confession is a strong deterrent that prevents a man from repeating a wrong doing.

Jesus son of Sirach says: "Do not be ashamed to confess your sins." (Sir 4:26)

A person should push himself to enter by the narrow gate. One should not be embarrassed to confess but should attain a clear conscience as the Holy Spirit takes away sins and puts them on Jesus Christ who carries all the sins of the world. It is through the sacrament of confession that we all gain forgiveness. (Eph 1:7; Col 1:14; Heb 7:25; 1 John 1:9; and 1 John 2:1,2)

WHAT DID THE FATHERS SAY?

St Isaac the Syrian says: "Do you work only when you feel like working or do you make an effort even if you do not feel like working? Compulsion to work is very important in both worldly and spiritual manners. It is important for prayer, reading spiritual books, and attending spiritual services in church. Do not obey your lazy body which is full of sin. The body wants to rest all the time as it does not bother about eternal destruction."

He also says: "The more a person struggles and forces himself for the sake of God, a heavenly support will surround him to facilitate his struggle and clear the way in front of him. Up until death, one should force himself for the sake of the Lord. It is better to die in struggle than to live in failure."

A person should not be lazy. He should force himself to pray even if he does not feel like praying. A person should force himself into spiritual practices, even during times of spiritual drought.

St. Ephram the Syrian says: "Pour tears in front of God so that your prayers become as incense. Water subsides a fire and tears put off an evil lust." St John Climacus says: "A weeping eye is a constant basin for the baptism of repentance and renewal."

Therefore, if forcing oneself is necessary in prayer, it is also necessary in fasting. There are many blessings to be gained from fasting. What then is our fathers' experience regarding fasting and the narrow gate?

St. Macarius the Great says: "Long suffering is patience; patience is victory; victory is life; life is kingdom and kingdom is God. The well is deep but its water is clear and fresh. The gate is narrow and the way is difficult but the city is full of happiness and joy. The tower is high and strong but it has precious treasures inside. Fasting is hard but it takes you to the heavenly kingdom. Doing good is not easy but it saves you from hell by the mercy of Our Almighty God."

St Pachomius, the father of community, says: "What a prize for those who were patient in temptations. All teachers, fathers, and the holy books command us to have great patience. The saints were patient and received the promises. Continue in prayer and fasting and do not be bored. Accept any suffering and the Lord will lift it from you. The Lord will not forget any of your effort while fasting."

St Isaac the Syrian says: "Every struggle against sin and its lusts should start with fasting especially in the struggle against internal sin."

He also says: "When our good Saviour was baptized, He was led by the Spirit to the desert where He fasted forty days and forty nights. All those who want to follow His steps should start their struggle in the same way."

St. Jerome answers those who object to fasting: "It is better that your stomach is ill than your soul be sick. Your knees may be shaken but not your chastity, so you better subdue your body than fall into temptation."

As for spiritual readings, especially the Holy Bible, it is necessary to read it because the Word of God is the best support to man during time of struggle. St Paul says: "For whatever things were written before were written for our learning, that we through the patience and comfort of the Scriptures might have hope." (Rom 15:4)

The Principle of the narrow gate in problems in life

There are many problems that face a person in his life. Some of these problems may be solved, while others require entry by the narrow gate. We will not go into detail here but will briefly mention few of these problems:

Family Problems:

This refers to problems of marriage and divorce. This is a wide subject but we will only briefly tackle it. It is very easy for either partner of a married couple to break the tie of marriage and approach family courts to obtain a divorce.

As per the Lord Jesus' law, divorce is only acceptable in case of adultery. A marriage could be saved if the one who is hurt by his partner carried the Cross and entered by the narrow gate. Those who ask for divorce as a quick solution for a marriage problem are not following Christ's command and consequently face many sorrows and heartaches. Their children suffer too.

Work Problems:

There are many problems in the work place. Problems in employment, in obtaining a higher position or a senior role, and in work transfer from one place to another. A person who feels that he was treated unfairly may do something wrong such as fall into anger, blaming others or envy. This may also lead to physical problems such as high blood pressure, heart attack or severe psychological problems.

If a person follows the steps of his Master and voluntarily enters the narrow gate, he will gain the blessings of tolerance and patience and all the promises that the Lord promised those who are persecuted for the sake of His Name. A person who is treated unjustly must be sure that the Lord Jesus is accompanying him as he carries his cross and enters by the narrow gate. He must be sure that the Lord will compensate him with many material and spiritual blessings.

In such cases, it is beneficial to look to Jesus, "He was oppressed and He was afflicted, yet He opened not His mouth." (Is 53:7) Let us remember what He said: "A disciple is not above his teacher, nor a servant above his master...If they persecuted Me, they will also persecute you...For if they do these things in the green wood, what will be done in the dry?" (Matt 10:24; John 15:20; Luke 23:31)

God will not leave injustice to prevail as if there is no God caring for the universe. Listen to what David the prophet says: "Do not fret because of evildoers, Nor be envious of the workers of iniquity. For they shall soon be cut down like the grass, and wither as the green herb. Trust in the LORD, and do good; Delight yourself also in the LORD, and He shall give you the desires of your heart. Commit your way to the LORD, trust also in Him, and He shall bring it to pass. He shall bring forth your righteousness as the light, and your justice as the noonday. Rest in the LORD, and wait patiently for Him; Do not fret because of him who prospers in his way,... Cease from anger, and forsake wrath; Do not fret—it only causes harm. For evildoers shall be cut off; but those who wait on the LORD, They shall inherit the earth. For yet a little while and the wicked shall be no more; indeed, you will look carefully for his place, but it shall be no more. But the meek shall inherit the earth, and shall delight themselves in the abundance of peace." (Psalm 37:1-11)

PAIN OF SICKNESS

Accepting the cross of sickness is a narrow gate that has its reward. It was said that one of the saintly fathers saw four levels in heaven: The first is a sick person patiently accepting his sickness with thanksgiving to God. The second is a healthy person looking after the foreigners and the weak. The third is the one struggling alone in the desert and the fourth is a disciple totally obeying his spiritual father. A thanksgiving patient presents his body daily as a sacrifice to God. The departed father Bishoy Kamel, the priest of St George Church, Sporting, Alexandria, was suffering from the pains of cancer and he used to smile and say: "This is the disease of paradise!!"

WORLDLY ATTRACTIONS AND WHAT IT HIDES:

There are numerous attractions in our world and they all hide many dangers. Our saintly fathers saw the wide easy way but they chose the narrow gate, knowing that all good things are behind it. The Lord Jesus is waiting for His beloved at the narrow gate. The Lord Jesus is waiting to walk the difficult path with you because its rewards and blessings are without measure. The following story was written in the Paradise of the Holy Fathers. It is about an old monk who was living in the desert. He used to draw water from a well which was far from where he lived by twelve miles. One time while he was going to draw water, he was annoyed and said to himself: "Why am I tiring myself? Let me live near the well." While he was thinking about this, he saw an old man behind him counting his steps. He asked him: "Who are you?" He replied: "I am the angel of God, sent to count your steps so that the Lord may reward your effort!!" When the old monk heard this, he was glad and increased the distance that he walked by another five miles.

www.ingramcontent.com/pod-product-compliance
Lightning Source LLC
LaVergne TN
LVHW091303080426
835510LV00007B/371